Published in 2018 by I Am Jen Wilson

Second Edition (First Edition: Become a Warrior Woman,
9 Rules to Sort Your Shit)

Jen Wilson has asserted her right to be identified as the
author of this Work in accordance with the Copyright,
Designs and Patents Act 1988

ISBN Paperback: 978-0-9957070-4-7

To:

My Soulmates

Contents   Page

The Creation Story

I believe that the ultimate goal in life for us is to be happy, and that is why I have written this book, '9 Rules to Sort Your Shit'. What 'happy' means to me is living a life with purpose with all its ups and downs.

This is the book's second edition, the first being 'Become a Warrior Woman, 9 Rules to Sort Your Shit'. I have dropped 'becoming a warrior woman' for a few reasons. One was I felt I had moved into a different phase of my journey, which no longer resonated.

There was a time in my life when I felt lost, stuck, and living in Groundhog Day and overwhelmed was holding me back. When I started working with my clients, I discovered they felt like that too. Or, in other words, we felt shit. The fact that you are reading this book suggests you may be in that same place. Good news; you are not alone, and the rules of this book will help.

I have overcome some exciting challenges in my life so far, and I am also continually working on the new ones that are thrown my way. The challenges keep us on our toes, learning, and growing as humans.
Through this book, I am going to share with you; how to get unstuck, how to understand who you are, how to find ways to love yourself, learn that it is okay to be selfish (from the positive meaning of the word), understand masculine and feminine energy and harmonise it within yourself, how to deal with stress, how to recognise valuable and useless procrastination, how to overcome self-sabotage, teach you about intuitive and mindful eating (which as the chapter says, eat the cake if you want to) and how to let go of the things that are holding you back.

I am Jen Wilson, The Healing Rebel, author, founder and creator of the Warrior Woman Project®, urban hippy, and Body, Mind & Soul coach.

From this very first chapter, please take full responsibility for everything you think about while reading this book and every action (or non-action) you take as a consequence.

Why do I ask you for that sort of commitment?
If you want to sort your shit, then it is up to you to make that happen. This book is a practical guide to get you started. There are action points and tasks to do throughout the book. Either get a notebook to write out your 'stuff', or you can buy the accompanying workbook that goes with this book.

I will take a stab in the dark that you are looking for some life-changing answers... unless you have stumbled across it by accident - I see that as a sign from the universe.

To give you a bit of my background and how this all came about, this part of my story starts on 21st September 2010 with this guy (Brian, now a close friend) who came to talk at my college about NLP (neurolinguistics programming). NLP is a life-changing way of reprogramming the brain so that we deal with the world more helpfully. It also helps you let go of the limiting beliefs that can hold you back from being the best version of yourself. Little did I know when I sat in that classroom listening to his stories that something I heard would drastically change my life.

Less than 2 weeks after that day, I had a life-changing conversation with my husband that would end our marriage and have him move back to Australia (his homeland). A year previously, I had already had a conversation with my best friend Grant that I thought things were going to end, it wasn't what I wanted, and I couldn't get the conversation to flow.

This new conversation, though, was different; we had both reached the ultimate pain point. He was unhappy and homesick and wanted to move back to Australia, and the reason we had moved back to Scotland was because I had been homesick in Australia. There was no way to work around it; there was no compromise workable. So to stay together, one of us would have to have been unhappy, which would only have caused more resentment later. Relationships can't work on those terms.

My whole life, as I knew it, was torn apart. Logically the split was understandable. There was no hate or fallout, and that made it more difficult. I, being me, told the world I was 'fine'; it was the 'right thing for both of us'- which was true. Of course, my 'fine' was a lie; I didn't think I had the right to be upset, and showing emotions wasn't something I did. So, I held it together by partying my nights away, spending my days busy with college work, setting up a business with my friend, working out, eating junk food, and having beers for breakfast on the days I didn't need to drive... For about 9 months, there was a lot of denial, distraction and numbing. I refused to (and also didn't think I needed to) let myself grieve. My denial that I was anything other than 'fine' came to a breaking point, and then there were tears and lots of them. I even got fed up with my own crying. My head was all over the place; I just wanted to be alone so I didn't need to talk to anyone. Everything was spinning, and I couldn't get a thought straight in my head. That was when I started to get some NLP coaching and gradually put my life back together.

This wasn't the first time I had been through a significant change in my life, but it was the first time I felt I needed a helping hand to get through it all. Admitting you need someone to help you and asking for it can feel like a massive challenge, especially if you have always been someone who has managed to sort your head out on your own in the past.

About 18 months before my divorce, I went through a career change. After spending 13 years in the travel industry, I was no longer inspired or motivated and knew I needed to do something drastic to change it. Life then felt so tricky; I didn't want to go to work, and it was depressing to get out of bed; some days, I really struggled to get through the day without thinking, 'Is this really all I have to look forward to for the rest of my life?' There are many stages in life when those questions come up 'Have I taken the right path?', 'Is this it?', 'am I missing out on something exciting?' 'Am I too old to make changes?' The answer to that last question is no, you are not too old, and it's not too late; not until you take your last breath is it too late to decide where your happiness is concerned.

Since the first edition of this book came out, I was diagnosed with Crohn's disease (which is a whole other book on its own). So it's yet another challenge to overcome where the rules in this book have helped.

I didn't know it then, but that talk Brian gave in 2010 and the conversation with my now ex-husband was the birthplace of the Warrior Woman Project® and the 9 Rules to Sort Your Shit.
Initially, I realised that I could help other women who, like me, felt challenged by changing their lives but know that it is something we must do. Then men started requesting guidance, so I edited this edition to be more gender-neutral.
I faced challenges through my divorce and the complete change in my career at 30. This helped me understand and shape my work into something easy to follow. It's practical and adaptable to different situations through my experience and the clients I have worked with.

Welcome to your journey.

My brand ethos is about exploring who you are, who you want to be, who you show up as in the world and the masks you hide behind.

We all have stuff we are happy to show and stuff we should hide. Those things that you hide are vulnerabilities that bring us the most connection.

In sharing my divorce story, partying ways, and even my Crohn's journey, people see that I am not a completely put-together, flawless human. I am flawed and not afraid to share that (anymore). Maybe flawed isn't the right word... Perhaps it's just human.

I talk a lot about learning to be selfish; let me acknowledge this word 'selfish'; I can already feel some of you gasping, screwing up your nose or pulling away, but stay with me for a minute so I can explain.

Think of yourself as a glass full of the most delicious drinking water, and you share some of that water with your family, friends, boss, partner, neighbour, and pet. You give, give, give, but you don't take any time to go to the tap to refill (you are just too busy with all the give, give, give)... You run out of water, you are thirsty, you get cranky, you snap at people, you can be irrational, you are moody, and you make crappy decisions that are generally out of character. Your glass is empty.

This is where your selfishness comes in; you learn to stop and refill your glass so you can get a drink, too, and that way, you can keep sharing and keep giving, and everyone wins. Not everyone will be happy when you take the time to refill, especially if you have been a giver up until now. You will even feel a bit guilty at first, but once you take the time, you feel better; the people you give to see you better then feel better, and everyone is happier, and the guilt and expectations can go.

It is the same as when they tell you on the plane to fit your oxygen mask first... You are no use to anyone if you are not breathing.

So, that is what I mean about learning to be selfish. Take some time to refill your glass, and look after yourself. Not only are you setting a good example to people around you, but you are also setting standards of how you need to live to survive happily in your world.

I've been there with the empty glass. I wasn't just a moody cow; I hit total burnout. I kept telling myself that I didn't need any time off because I loved everything I did (work hard, play hard, you can sleep when you are dead kind of nonsense), and it made me happy doing things for everyone else. But, I was numbing myself from the reality of my marriage ending, keeping so busy there wasn't time to think or feel. Then I landed on my ass and couldn't get out of bed for nearly 2 weeks. So I will go into that more in the chapter on self-sabotage.

This used to be a much bigger problem for women than men, but in recent years I am seeing more and more men burning out trying to meet society's expectations. These expectations are bullshit created by marketing companies and are out there to make us feel insignificant and buy more crap that we are told will make us happier. It won't.
In the process of recovery from my burnout, I had to make a lot of 'selfish' decisions, they weren't easy, and it didn't happen overnight. I had to cut ties with people, give up teaching many of my fitness classes and close down 2 businesses that I owned with a friend; I had to take time off, learn to deal with my shit and look after myself better (eating the right foods, and doing the right kind of exercise for me at that time).

Part of that journey was about taking responsibility for myself and my life; it was time for me to realise what I was capable of, stop hiding behind others, set up on my own and work to a new set of rules I created. I had worked my ass off to gain all these qualifications, and now I needed to do something with them. For someone who really didn't like education the first time around, I now have a BSc in Sport and Exercise Science, PGDip Teaching in Further Education (TQFE) qualification, an NLP Master Practitioner, Pilates, Yoga, Meditation teacher and massage therapist (among many other fitness qualifications I have gained along the way).

I could only take that career change and step back into education because I put my happiness first; I realised that I wanted to help people in a much deeper way than booking their holidays. So I tried to make a real impact and difference in the world.

I knew I needed to help people who felt lost and stuck in the world. We worked hard to create that life throughout our 20s and now think we want something different. What you have created so far doesn't need to be IT for the rest of your life.

I took my time working it out; I've learned about meditation and its power to bring ideas to you. The concept of Warrior Woman Project® came to me one day after morning meditation, as did the idea for the first edition of this book – I love how stuff like that happens when you are not even thinking about it. It's the unconscious mind working its magic. And, through meditation, we can find the quiet space we need to hear.

At the start, I used to write a daily blog telling my story and suggesting different ways to think about the world and deal with life. Within a couple of months, my mailing list had more than doubled, and I was getting responses from readers asking how I knew what was happening in their heads? Was I a mind reader? I had reached into their hearts and understood exactly where they were and that I knew just the right thing to say at the right time. A few people had suggested I condense the best ideas into a book, and here it is.

The thing about those blogs was I was writing about what I had either been through, was going through or what I could see happening with the people close to me.

We are all going through 'stuff'. We all have doubts and insecurities, and we need those words, a different point of view or a task that makes us think differently to potentially realise our strengths and capabilities.

The mission of my business is to create a community of people who empower themselves and each other, so they live a life that not only makes them happy but also inspires those around them to do the same. We aim to set an example of self-management, leadership and responsibility for everyone in the communities we are connected to. We want to create a ripple effect.

The feedback I've had from clients from reading the book, attending workshops, listening to the podcast, completing online programmes and doing one-to-one coaching sessions has been phenomenal. Changes are happening. Confidence is being built. New jobs are being applied for. New countries are being lived in. These people are starting to understand their importance and that they could give more by being happy in more areas of their life. There is genuine happiness in these people's lives, and they're sharing it.

So we must make changes in ourselves before we can change the bigger world.

There will still be some struggles and setbacks, we are human, and life likes to throw us a curveball from time to time to remind us that what happens around us is out of our control. What we do have is control over how we react. Resilience gets stronger every time we get back up, to the point where sometimes we can see that the curve ball knocking us off balance is actually fun.

The people working with me through all the different channels are setting an example, realising their worth and feeling happier every day. I am not going to bullshit you and tell you they woke up the next day completely changed; it's hard work and takes effort; they have to face new challenges and let go of the shit they have been using as their security blanket. They must let go of 'it's not my fault' and 'poor me' excuses.
They've taken responsibility for their lives, actions and happiness. They stopped waiting for someone else to come and save the day.

From this experience, I've created a structure and formula that works. 9 Rules to Sort Your Shit.

The message is simple; you can be whoever you want to be and have everything you need to sort your shit and create the ripple effect. All you need to do is start with you. Realise you can only change yourself, lead by example and always do your best.

This leads me to the very first exercise of the book (yip straight in there in chapter one); it is entirely up to you how you work this, some of you might love to buy a notebook or get the 9 Rules to Sort Your Shit workbook (available from Amazon) or make use of the spaces left within the book, and others might want to have a think about it and not actually write anything.

*I strongly advise and encourage you to write your responses and ideas from each exercise. Not only do you then have a note of this, but you also will find it more powerful having written it and create a stronger connection with your thoughts, your mind and your future actions.

Exercise

You will notice that the Wheel of Happiness has no headings filled in for you.

I do this because the generic ones are good, but some of the headings can be further broken down or irrelevant.
I suggest making a couple of copies of the wheel (there are 12 to use in the workbook) and doing one general using headings: Personal Development, Relationships, Health, Career/Work, Money, Fun, Family, Spirituality/Religion.

Then, for any with more than one meaning or want to break down further, select headings that are most relevant to you. For example, let's say Relationships score a 5; some of your relationships might be a 10, and some might be a zero – friends, family, romantic, work colleagues, and kids are all different relationships. Health could be physical, mental, emotional, fitness, nutrition, etc.

Other examples of headings that might be more relevant to you could be:

Body image, weight, food, religion, spirituality, money, career, personal development, health, social life, attitude, environment (your own living and working space), the global environment, hobbies, fun, time management, etc...

If some other headings or words resonate better, use them; these are just examples.

0 = despair, you need serious change 10 = delirious, there is nothing that could make it better.

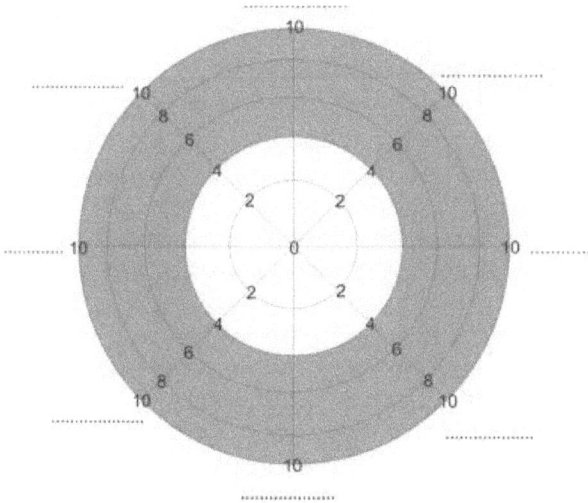

It is helpful to date and hold on to your wheel to compare each time you evaluate (I recommend monthly).

It is also helpful to remember that the wheel reflects where you are in your head at the present time. For example, if you have had a horrible week at work or a fight with a family member, that might influence your score.

We're not looking for balance in the wheel. It would be impossible for us to achieve a 10 in all areas all of the time. If you consider that, like the calendar year, our life works in seasons. Sometimes, we need to focus more on our careers, meaning that our social life might need to be stepped back a bit. Or there might be a health issue that means you need to be with family more and take a step back from business.

Problems arise when we need to focus on one thing, but we prefer to focus on something else (e.g. your business needs attention, but you are choosing to socialise and procrastinate from the work you need to do). Don't worry if this is happening; we all do it... It is essential to recognise that we are doing it and take steps to get back on track.

Right now, all we are looking at is what is out of balance and checking in with ourselves whether or not it's okay for it to be out of balance. This is really important. If it's okay that it's out of balance, you don't need to give yourself a hard time. If it's not okay, now you can do something to implement a plan.

I need to work on myself daily, there are always things I can do better, more significant challenges to accept, improvements to be made, and facing up to something that I want to avoid, but over the years, I have come a long way. We need to leave a legacy that comes through hard work, living our passions, setting an example, never giving up on ourselves and never settling.

That day back in 2010, I listened, took action, made some massive decisions and changes to my life, and don't regret a single one. I now run a successful business, and I regularly take time to refill my cup so I can work hard, share the love and lead by example.

I hope you enjoy the journey.

Jen x

Action

- Breathe
- Accept responsibility for your actions
- Be honest with yourself, always
- Give yourself a break

Rule #1

Know who you are.

Feeling lost and unsure who you seem to be part of growing up – hopefully, it is good news for you to know that you are not alone and that at regular points in your life, we all go through it. When we first come into the world, we are happy and content with life, eating, sleeping, pooing, and learning as we watch the world go by. We are influenced by what we see and hear. At some point, we start questioning ourselves or changing to try and fit in. These then become transitional phases. Remember when you started high school? Transitioning through your teen years into your early 20s when you might have dabbled with different styles, groups of friends, music, interests, hobbies etc.

Thinking back, we might have seemed more open to trying and testing out new things that we maybe think twice about now that we are 'adulting'... How many arguments did you have with your parents about your hair colour, the amount of makeup you wore, the length of your skirt, wearing a tracksuit on Christmas day or that racket you call music?

If you have any interest or belief in astrology, then every 27-30 years, when Saturn returns to the point it was when you were born, it can cause shifts and changes in your life (and repeat again another 27-30 years later). I definitely felt like I was having a crisis. So in that age bracket, I moved to Australia, moved back home from Australia, divorced, bought a house, had a complete career change and went back into full-time education... I went for all the upheaval!

You may think you should feel more settled in life as you age. Indeed as you grow up, you will find your 'place' in the world, and you shouldn't have to make so many difficult decisions. As a kid, you probably couldn't wait to grow up, and now, as a grown-up, you possibly wish you were still a kid when life was more straightforward. Saying that I would not enjoy being a kid in today's world with the pressures of social media. I appreciate the lessons I had before the internet existed.

At this time, as an adult, we are more aware of changes and unsettled feelings going on, and we may feel less equipped to deal with them, but please be reassured we have the skills to get through what might feel like an overwhelming time. I will show you how with these 9 Rules to Sort Your Shit.
It's time to introduce you to Rule #1 and introduce yourself to you.

I believe 'Just be yourself' has to be the worst advice ever given to anyone... How often have you heard the advice 'Just be yourself, you are fabulous, people will love you just the way we do', 'You have nothing to worry about',' If only you could see yourself the way I see you?

Whenever I heard these statements, I thought, 'Yeah, no problem, but... WHO THE HELL AM I???' How do you see me? How can you be yourself if you are not entirely who you are or what you want from life?

'Just take the mask off and expose the real you'. That is another mind-blowing statement... Real me?? I didn't know there wasn't a real me...

The thing about masks is we have many of them, and they are all the real us. We have our work mask, our socialising with work mask, our socialising with friends mask, our spending time with the extended family mask, our first date mask, our dealing with difficult people masks, our dancing round the house naked mask, our singing at the top of our lungs in the car mask... We have many masks that we wear depending on the situation we face. They are all you.

A problem can arise when we feel really comfortable in one mask and use it as our protection to hide behind. Maybe you kick ass at work and use that same approach with friends and at home, never backing down, always being the boss, and never showing emotion.

Or there is the parent who is there for the kids 24/7 making sure everything is just right for them, making their decisions, getting them organised, and treating all their family and friends in the same way, for want of a better phrase, 'ring' everyone around them.

Or maybe you are the one that is always ready to party. When everyone is looking for a drinking buddy or a night out to get wasted, you are the one they call on. Everyone knows you are the first one to the bar and the last one standing, and the party's back at your house.

Maybe you are asking, 'Who do you think I am if I am not the person standing in front of you right now?!'

Every time you are being you, you are being you... Let me explain. In the car, when you are singing your heart out (if you are me, entirely out of tune), that is you. When you are in the boardroom, kicking ass and controlling the room, that's also you. So when you are in the supermarket doing your weekly shopping, yip, that's also you... Whatever you are doing, it's always a version of you... I am not sure how it would go down if you were in a meeting singing your heart out instead of kicking ass... At the core of all these versions of you are your values, what is most important to you.

We have many masks (or hats or labels, whatever you prefer to call them), and each has a specific role in helping us through the day and fitting into the situation at that time.

These masks we wear daily give us some protection and allow us to adapt to whatever situation we are dealing with. They allow us to tap into different parts of our personality and strengths to help us win in life.

So, who the hell are you? Who do you want to be? And what the hell are these values?

Sometimes the masks that can give us protection also can hold us back. We are never far from an excuse for our behaviours; 'I can't have a career because I am a mum'. 'I don't have time to be in a relationship; I am too busy focusing on my career'. Or 'I'm fat because I'm a chocoholic'... whatever the reason, the excuses are ready.

So...If you were to overhear someone talking about you, what would you LIKE to hear them say about you? Do you feel like you are that person? How do you show up in the world?

Very probably, you are at the heart and soul of yourself, but do you let the world see that person so that when they talk about you, these are the things they say?

On the other side, who do you hope they don't see you as? We often try to hide our vulnerabilities and are usually the reason for the mask.

The exciting thing I have learned over the last decade is that our vulnerabilities help us connect to each other as humans.

Exercise

Who would you be if you had the choice to be anyone in the world?

What would you be like?

What would you do?

How would you talk?

How would you dress?

What would your behaviours be like?

What would you achieve in life?

What image do you want to portray to the rest of the world?

What would happen in your world to make you happy every day?

Are there people you would like to be more like in your world?

Bonus Exercise

Reflected Best Self

Email 15-20 people you know and know reasonably well (in all different areas of your life) and ask them what they see when you are your best self.

As they reply, collect the information and compare it to find common threads.

It will be a great week receiving emails.

The traits that we see in others, whether we like them or not, are what we recognise in ourselves. All the positive attributions that draw them to you are all positive attributions you have in you. Maybe you know that, or you might need to work on your confidence to bring it out more – don't worry, we will get to that later in the book.

I remember the first time I learned this; I was mortified that I was drawn to someone for their big heart, confidence, happiness, natural beauty and authenticity. When I looked in the mirror, I didn't see that person immediately; I had to learn to see her and that it was okay to appreciate positive attributes of myself. So who was I to think I had a big heart, confidence, happiness, natural beauty and authenticity!? I will discuss this more later in a rule about self-love and self-belief.

Part of settling into yourself is to understand who you want to be. Creating a 'To Be' list rather than a 'To Do' list can massively help. How do you show up 'to be'? That is what that first exercise is about. The mask you have on now fills a role you may have fallen into but hadn't been your lifelong plan. Somewhere along the road, you continued to take time and reassess what and who you wanted to be going forward.
As a kid, maybe you dreamed of exploring the world, but after school, you went to university and landed an excellent job. The opportunity was too good to miss... Or you met the partner of your dreams young, got married, and had kids but really wish you had the chance to go to university... Or maybe you went off travelling and are now finding it difficult to 'settle' into a 'normal' life - whatever that is!

The next part we are going to look at helps you understand what your core values are. Your To Be list will help you pick these values out. These are the character traits we live by, and when we live by the ones most important to us, decision-making is more manageable, and we feel happier and more settled. Understanding your core values makes it a lot easier to learn how to 'just be you' no matter which role you are in.

I remember the first time values were discussed in an NLP coaching session. I looked blankly at Brian thinking, 'Is this another one of these questions I don't want to answer? Is this going to make me cry?' – It didn't; it cleared a whole lot of stuff up; it was a real lightbulb moment. So taking the time to work out my values in life, career, relationships and, more recently, money has helped me work better overall.

I quickly discovered that this was something I NEEDED to know and have been very grateful for ever since, as have all my clients when I have worked through this task with them. I have my lists written out and put in place. I see them regularly as a reminder, especially when I struggle to decide. I bring my attention back to the values that help give some clarity. Listen to your gut instincts. If that isn't something you are well practised in, it might take some time - it's practice.

When things feel like they don't sit right with us, we feel uneasy about decisions that have been made. For example, actions or attitudes from others feel wrong, problems arise, and a horrible unsettled feeling can stir up, and that is usually when our values are not being met, and life is going against our values system. When we are clashing with other people, it usually means that our values are out of alignment. This can be useful to know and understand to help you better work with challenging situations.

So what are values, and how do we work out our own?

Core values are the things that are important to you, not what society thinks you should be (don't confuse morals with values). They are the feelings that, whether or not you are aware of them, you make your life decisions around. When something feels utterly right with you, it is because it meets your values; when something doesn't feel right with you, it doesn't. The four main areas but not exclusive, that I encourage you to know your values are: life, career, relationships and money.

Exercise

Working out your values:

You can download a table of example values at www.iamjenwilson.com/resources to use - remember that list is not exhaustive; there are no right or wrong answers, and you can add or change any of the words you like. They need to mean something to you.

If you are using that list, sit for a maximum of 3 minutes (the time it) and highlight the ones that jump out at you and make you think, ', Yes, that is really important to me'. Then, write out a list of your highlighted ones, narrow this down to your top 10, and then put them in order of most to least important.

If you want to avoid using the template with the examples, with a blank sheet of paper, write down the feelings that are most important to you; once you have a list of 10-12 words, put them in order of importance. Don't worry if you get stuck for words; keep thinking, keep asking yourself, 'What else is important to me?' You might end up with a few words with similar meanings; check with yourself if they mean the same thing to you or if they are different, e.g. Trust and honesty. To some people, these are the same; to others, they are entirely different. If they are the same, keep the one that resonates most with you. If they mean different things and are both critical, keep both.

Knowing and understanding YOUR definition of each word you select is essential. Take the time to do all 4 areas: life, career, relationships and money. The 4 lists may be very similar (or not at all – remember there is no right and wrong, it's about what works for you); it might just be their order of them is different. So, for example, for some people in their careers, values and security might be high up on the list of values, but in relationships, that might be low or non-existent or vice versa.

Tip: write them out on individual Post-it notes so you can quickly move and change the order, or the sheet of paper could get pretty messy, or do it in a Word or Excel document if you prefer (I like old school paper).

Once you have your list and definitions, please read it, and start to understand where these fit in your life and why they are important to you; look at your life and how they work around your values. Don't make the values fit around your life. The decisions you make in life are because of these values. When something doesn't feel right, it is usually because something goes against your values.

Let's look at how this works for you. Say commitment was high on your relationship values; the person you see wants to keep things casual and open. You might first agree to see how it goes, but it won't feel good if it stays that way for a long time and doesn't seem to be moving on to a committed relationship. You won't feel happy about it; you might even feel insecure about yourself. That's because the casual arrangement goes against a core value. If the other person doesn't want the commitment, that's not about you being undesirable or not good enough; it's about you having different values that are not aligned.

If honesty is up there in your lists, a political career will likely be out because any mistruth will really piss you off.

You might be really honest, but would the people around you be, and can you be okay with that?

Once you start living by your values, you will not be happier, but better things will happen; you will feel more settled and like you finally understand yourself. Your life will be easier; making decisions will be easier because you know the 'what and why' of your decision-making. The different masks you wear in your roles will all have more meaning and understanding, and switching between them will be easier. You don't need to protect yourself so much by hiding in your comfort zone.

Try not to stress about your lists, these are not set in stone, and you can review them anytime. Understanding them should give you peace and freedom in your thinking. At another time, another word will come to you that fits better, and you can change it. Also, as the balance in your life changes, their order may change too. Reviewing and revisiting this task if you feel like the world isn't fitting anymore to see what's changed is good practice. Your life situations change, and your values may shift as you grow.

This task is about helping you learn and understand how to be the real deal so you can indeed 'just be yourself' no you are wearing.

Now that you understand yourself better, it can also help you know the people around you better. If there are people that you clash with all the time, it could be that your values are not aligned, and understanding this allows you to adapt and manage them or the situation better – you can't expect the other person to adapt if they are not in a place of working on themselves or interested in being adaptable. So it might not be in line with their values. But of course, you could always give them the gift of this book, but in the meantime, you are responsible for being adaptable now that you have a better understanding.

We have to remember that the only person we can control is ourselves, and that means that we have to control how we respond to situations.

Action

- Breathe
- Accept responsibility for your actions
- Be honest with yourself, always
- Give yourself a break
- Work out your values for life, career, relationships & money
- Know and understand your values (have them written in a diary or somewhere you can easily access them)
- Be aware of other people's values when there is a conflict and understand where they are coming from
- Review them regularly to make sure that they are still relevant
- Do what feels right for you, not what you think other people expect of you

Rule #2

Dreams & goals, know what you want

I spent much time through my school years daydreaming (and in adult life, I still love a good daydream). I was generally uninspired and disengaged with the school system for most of my school life. I was there because I was supposed to be. I was never a troublemaker, but I did get told off quite a bit for not paying attention, and my report cards always had the 'competent' box checked. Two high school teachers sparked my interest, my 1st-year art teacher Miss Wilson and my 1st-year history and modern studies teacher Mr Snee. I don't know what it was about them or those classes, but I did well in them; I paid attention and got good marks... Unfortunately, that was the only year I had either of them, and after that, I would sit down in class and mentally check out, dreaming about what life would be like when I was a grown-up and could make my own decisions.

I was often told I had my 'head in the clouds' or that my 'head was full of broken biscuits'. It made no difference; I just floated back into my world, thinking, okay, whatever.

The first thing I did when I walked out the school gates on the last day was chucking all my books in the bin... I was going to college to study travel and tourism and then get to see the world...

Much to my surprise, I did really well at college. In fact, I got student of the year! I asked the senior lecturer if she had the right person when she phoned to tell me. I had never been top of the class, never mind the top of 60 college students! That first award of recognition made me realise that I could, in fact, do more with my life and that my school years were not the big set-up for a life that they had been made out to be. So many people say your school years are the best of your life, which makes me sad. That makes me think they have stopped living, dreaming, and believing there is more to life.

If the purpose of life is to live a happy life, and we are not here for a long time, the only certainty is we will die. We need to do the things that make us happy plus all the other stuff in between – getting up, washing, eating, doing the dishes, maybe dealing with people we might not love to deal with, or doing things that might not set our soul on fire. But, what we do around that, where we find joy in everyday things, is where we get the big wins in life.
Being grateful that we wake up and have the skills and capabilities to wash, eat, do the dishes, communicate... We need to be grateful for everything we take for granted daily.

Our dreams are the motivation to move us towards being happy. We set goals to help us fulfil those dreams. Let me put something straight; we will fail at parts of our journey. We need to, or we are not living. Sometimes those failures will be minor bumps in the road (how do you find the cash to travel?), or they can be a fork in the road where you have to decide one way or the other (do we stay married or go our separate ways?) or they can seem like unclimbable mountains (I don't have the skills, knowledge, time, finances, or faintest idea how to start my own business). The critical thing to remember is you need to regroup and go again. To understand what is important to you, go to your values, think about what else could and didn't work before, try something else, and ask for help. You are absolutely allowed to ask for help.

When you get the conditions right, you will succeed, and very few of us, very few times, will get it right the first time (that is good news). Only as we get older do we have a problem with failing at things. Watch a baby, see how often they try something and fail and try again...Would you ever let that baby give up trying to walk? Failing is how we grow and develop. At no point does anyone ever tell the baby to stop trying; they have tried enough... Try again, and again, and again, always encouraging them. At that age, the embarrassment of failure isn't something we are even aware of existing; we learn that a few years later at nursery or school and then most of us let that fear to hold us back.

Don't let other people's judgement hold you back.

Do you have a big dream? Don't worry if you don't; I will get to that.

I saw Colonel Chris Hadfield speak in Edinburgh; his tour was called The Sky is Not the Limit... I love that title.

The stand-out point for me, which I had never heard anyone else say, was that it really doesn't matter if you never achieve the dream, but if you do everything you can to work towards that dream, you won't ever live a life disappointed.

This was a revolutionary and profound moment for me... 'it doesn't matter if you never achieve that dream' Who knew?!

Permission had just been granted to dream even bigger than I imagined possible, and it would be okay if I didn't get there... If you are following the path to the dream, then you are always going to be doing things for a reason, and they will usually be things that you enjoy – I am not sure when I was sitting for hours writing essays for uni would have said I was enjoying it, but I always knew there was a purpose to the action and that makes the difference.

One of the many amazing and successful women I know runs dance schools for kids and shared one day about the success of her business and how a teacher at school had told her dance wasn't a real job and that she should do something real... Thankfully she ignored that teacher who followed her dream and is reaping the success of her hard work.

There will always be people who will encourage you to give up on your dreams or tell you that what you want is out of reach...
DON'T LISTEN TO THEM! Maybe they gave up on their dreams; perhaps they believed someone when told that... When you are told things like 'don't be too big for your boots', 'know your place', or someone asks 'who do you think you are?' it can plant a seed of doubt in your mind, and that seed can be enough to hold you back. Does that give them the right to tell you that you can't or shouldn't chase your dreams? This is your life; it is up to you to take responsibility for it.

How much happier will you be if you do everything you can to be the person you want to be?

To be a top surgeon, you must attend medical school, work through the ranks, departments, and courses, and shadow other top surgeons. There is no point settling for a course in accounting because that is your best subject at school.

If you want to be a movie star, you need to get in front of the camera, get those parts as extras, go to the auditions, and put yourself in situations where you might get your break.
To succeed, you must create the right conditions to make the results happen. To create the right conditions, you need to set some goals and to get those results, you need to understand why they are important to you.

Don't worry if you don't know; I am getting to that.

Start at the top; what is the big picture? What is the dream? If your life was picture perfect, what would that look like? Be honest; this is your dream. Then work your way back, breaking things down into smaller steps and goals, always with that dream in mind. Strip each step back, breaking it down until you get to a To Do list that doesn't terrify the life out of you. This can be the route plan to get you moving towards the dream.

In the first chapter, we looked at your Wheel of Happiness to see where we are in life; what is out of balance? How does that make you feel right now? Let's say your decided one of your headings was romantic relationships, and that was down at a 3 or 4; maybe that is okay for you because being in a romantic relationship is not a high priority to you... But perhaps part of your dream is to be happily married with children. This will change the importance of how and when you make this a focus in your life.

Now, if you don't know what the dream is, that is totally okay; some of us don't know; I am still trying to figure it out too. What are you curious about? Use your curiosities as a guide. Go and learn, try things out, and experience as much as possible.
Change it up when and if you decide it's not for you. Be bold and curious (some people might see it as flaky, but I don't, curiosity is not flaky). The more variety you have, the more likely you are to stumble over the things that make you feel alive. Sometimes the dream will find you. Otherwise, you are having experiences in your life and not settling.

It is much more common for my clients to have a blank expression when I ask them what their dream is and what they really want. There is often a mix of 'I don't know', 'I haven't really thought about it' or shyness about saying out loud what they want because they don't want to come across as selfish, egotistical or mad. Chris Hadfield was 9 when he knew he wanted to be an astronaut even though they had never, at that time, sent a Canadian into space. His whole education and career were focused on taking the necessary courses and steps to give him the proper education and skills just in case the time came that he could be sent up to space. His dreams came true; he was 33 before becoming actively involved in the space programme and 42 before getting to space.
Someone is going to be an astronaut, a prime minister, a president, a Royal Princess, a head teacher, a top surgeon, a supermodel, a multi-million-pound bra

designer, an award-winning actor, a bestselling author, or owner of the most recognisable brand in the world, Olympian... Why can that someone not be you?
Regular people do extraordinary things all the time. So many people we highly respect at the top of industries have once been 'normal' people like us, living life, making decisions, and working with the cards they were dealt.

Reading autobiographies and watching documentaries about people's lives can be a real eye-opener to the struggles and journeys many at the top of their game have been through.
Please don't worry if you sit there thinking, 'Oh, Jen, I have no idea what I want to do'. Remember when you were a kid, before 'the real world' killed your imagination; what did you love to do? What sparks your interest? What can you get lost doing for hours? Are you just scared to say it out loud? – don't worry; this is a book; I can't hear you.

If you genuinely don't know, put your question out to the universe and be open to the answer coming back to you. When you experience things you like, remember to thank the universe and ask for more of the same or better.

Tip: Meditate – most of my best ideas come to me during or after meditation. Before you panic about being unable to meditate, I have been there; I have read books, listened to apps, and been on the courses. The best advice I got was to focus on your breath. Even if it is for 2 breaths, your mind wanders, and you bring it back. Focus on 2 breaths, and your mind wanders. That is better than not trying or declaring meditation isn't for you. It doesn't need to be long; a few minutes daily will calm your mind. There will always be an internal dialogue; it's what the brain does.

Think about the brain like a snow globe shaken up, the glitter is your thoughts swirling everywhere, and you can't see the picture clearly. The way to let the glitter settle is to sit the globe still, and the picture becomes clear.

There are loads of apps, videos and classes. Test out a few until you find the one you like, and roll with that. You can mix and match.

Thoughts will pop into your head, and you will drift off, lost in your thoughts; as soon as you become aware, take your focus back to whatever your focus was on. If sitting still to breathe isn't your thing, then if you can get out for a walk, be present, look at the scenery, listen to the sounds and focus on your breathing there (leave your phone behind, unplug, no technology to distract you), fresh air and focused breathing will really clear your head.

A lot of this is about quieting down the distractions of life and letting your brain settle so you can let your thoughts through.

If nothing comes through to you during your meditation (or quiet time), keep doing it anyway, it's good for your mind, body and soul. Take your time.

Once you create an image of your dream, whether it's travel, career, relationships, health, interests, hobbies, or general life improvements, it can make the whole goal-setting and planning process more manageable.

When it comes to setting your goals, if you like to journal, you can review your plan every single day. I have friends that spend time focusing on their vision daily. My week could be more structured, and I find it challenging to review daily, so I check every 4 weeks (or the 1st of every month) and work with To Do lists in between. Whatever the frequency, make sure that it works for you, and not only are you on track to achieving your goals but also to make sure they are still the goals you want to achieve.

Sometimes your goals will change, and that is totally okay,

Have you ever applied for a job only to realise during the interview that it's not the right job for you? Or you start on a weight loss journey only to discover that eating cake every now and again is more important because it is part of your social life and that eating salad and vegetable sticks every day or counting points or sins sucks and you are missing out on a lifestyle that you actually enjoyed. Softness in your body is not the end of the world; if you love your body the way it is, that is way more important (more on that later in the book). Or, have you joined a gym only to realise that you hate being stuck indoors all the time and that structured exercise is not for you?

It's important to understand that just because you said you were going one way, it's okay to change your mind when you realise that what you thought would make you happy doesn't.

Nothing's set in stone; the outcome of any goal is to make you happy in the long term.

**Note here, sometimes some journeys are challenging; studying, training, portion control etc., can be a pain in the ass, but sometimes we have to make short-term sacrifices to gain long-term results. Always go back to your Why when it feels like a struggle. The struggle is real and part of your journey, making you stronger. Go back to your values; are you living by them?

Once you figure out what it is you want, you need to work out how you will get it. Some of the questions you will want to consider:

What do you need to do?
What are you prepared to sacrifice?
Who can you get to help you?
What are the financial costs?
What are the emotional costs?
Who else does it affect? Is it worth it?

It would be best if you also considered a contingency plan. Sometimes you are all set to go, and something gets in your way – the kids get sick, your boss or a client calls an unexpected emergency meeting, you don't get on to the course you want to get on... Plans then will need to change, but rather than giving up, you must do your best in the circumstances. So take a moment to consider 'What is the best way to deal with this situation?'

It's up to you to set your conditions to allow everything to come together. Call in help, get extensions on deadlines and identify other routes that you can take.

You need to put yourself into the right mindset, focus on your why and make sure that changes out of your control don't allow you to self-sabotage (self-sabotage is when you put obstacles in your own way and give yourself excuses to get out of things, e.g. the kids, the boss, clients, the weather etc.). Don't worry. We will go into this in detail in the next chapter.

Contingency examples:
You have packed your gym stuff, set the alarm, and prepared all your food ready to go first thing in the morning.

The alarms went off, you could hear the rain battering off the windows, and you didn't get the best sleep, so you decide that you are cosy in bed and won't get up for the gym but plan to go to the end of the day instead.

So, you get up later, then, during the day, nothing seems to go to plan, and then one of your friends calls and invites you to the pub after work.

You have 2 options here...

You can ditch the gym and head to the pub 'for one; you can start fresh tomorrow.
Or
You can thank your friend for the invite, but you promised yourself that the extra hour in bed was a

compromise for a post-work gym session. You can always invite your friend along to the gym.
Obviously, option 2 is the one that will keep you closer to your goal than option 1.

Life is full of temptations that take us off in other directions, sometimes, these occasional distractions are okay, but problems arise when it happens a lot. How often do you let that happen to you? I'll start tomorrow / Monday / when I get paid / when the kids are in bed... They are all excuses that delay the start and your potential success.

When something gets in the way, stick as close to the original plan as possible. Flexibility and resilience are essential skills to develop, and like muscles, they take work to get stronger.

Once you get on a roll, it is good to keep going, and I know that some people, if they fall out of routine, even for one day, can be knocked off for weeks. That's where your resilience needs training. Acknowledge if that is the type of person you are, and prepare to be strict with yourself to get back on track as soon as possible (or get a coach or friend to hold you accountable). So when you keep the focus on your values and your goals, it makes it so much easier to reign yourself back. So there comes a time in your life when you need to become responsible for your own actions.

As humans, our brains are wired to desire and seek familiarity; the unpredictable and unknown can make us feel unsafe. We unconsciously seek out familiar patterns, creating enough self-awareness to recognise those patterns and find ways to break the ones that no longer serve us. We often feel disappointed in ourselves when we recognise a pattern that has been 'harmful' or against our goals, but it's good to remember that we don't know what we don't know. Self-awareness is an ongoing journey.

Becoming self-aware can trigger the feeling of being overwhelmed, which can be numbing, make us feel dizzy, breathless, foggy-headed, even fearful... It can be so paralysing that it feels easier to settle with what you have rather than chase the dream. It can even have you questioning your goals and if it's really worth the hassle. It often happens when we look at the end result rather than the next step or create a vast to-do list with big tasks that we never tick off.

If we feel overwhelmed creeping in and consuming us, we must stop and take a breath. So often, our go-to behaviour is to do more... instead of less. Step away and give your head some space to think, organise, get clarity and plan. We need to remember that going after our dream is an act of bravery. You are standing up for yourself and not accepting a life of 'just okay'. Being brave and consistently taking steps toward your dream is the key to success here. It doesn't matter how small the action is; it's better than no step – sometimes, that step is taking a break and getting clarity. We admire resilient people... Be that person you admire.

When I first set the goal of writing this book, for the first draft, I sat in an internet café every Saturday for hours working, making progress, and fighting with my laptop as I seemed to get viruses uploaded on what felt like a daily basis and the flash drive didn't always save my work even though I religiously hit that save icon.

I got a notebook for the second draft and wrote most of it by hand before typing it up. I originally started working with a publisher and then changed direction to self-publish. When I sat down with the publisher, he told me he was sure I wouldn't be happy with the final edit because they wanted to 'water my voice down', which didn't fit with the ethos of my brand. So we don't water ourselves down to fit in. So I was very grateful for his honesty and help to that point.

During the writing process, I missed many beautiful days outside in the sun; I had to postpone plans and spend a fortune on tea to achieve this goal... If you are reading this book now, it means I successfully got the first edition out. The second edition still took dedication, but I got it done in a much shorter time because it was a read-through of the original text and making necessary changes.

To get the things we want in life, not only do we need to be prepared to fail, but we also need to be prepared to prioritise, compromise and miss out on some things.

Goal + Plan + Contingency + Determination = Success/ Dream

Exercise

You can download your Dream, Goal, Plan worksheet from www.iamjenwilson.com/resources or use the goal worksheets in the workbook (that you can purchase from Amazon if you haven't already).

Use your Wheel of Happiness from Chapter 1 and your values from Rule 1; these will help work out your goals for the next month.

If you use your phone or an online calendar, it can be helpful to set monthly reminders to review the wheel and goals. Check in to see if you are on track, still moving in the right direction, or want to achieve that outcome. If you use a manual calendar, get writing in it now to plan out the end of the year in it as a reminder to review. Whichever calendar you are using, schedule the time and stick to it.

Action

- Breathe
- Accept responsibility for your actions
- Be honest with yourself, always
- Give yourself a break
- Meditate
- Know or at least have an idea of what the big dream is
- If you can't think of a dream, follow your curiosities
- Do the things that make you happy
- Write out your dreams, this can be in a journal or on a vision board, whatever works best for you
- Never let anyone tell you your dream is ridiculous – it's your dream, not theirs
- Write out your goals
- Create a plan and a To Do list and action something on it every single day
- Even the smallest step is still a step

Rule #3

Quit with the excuses

In Chapter 3, I briefly mentioned the term self-sabotage. This is something many of us have mastered quite successfully, yet it is the thing that stops us from being who we want to be; it holds us back from chasing our dreams and finding true peace within ourselves. It's the excuse we use to not achieve what we say we want.

Probably the easiest way to explain self-sabotaging is with our diets because nearly everyone I have worked with struggles in this area, even if they don't struggle with their weight. Whether it is a new year's resolution, another Monday is rolling around, you have a holiday coming up or are just generally feeling crap about how you look or feel, we frequently self-sabotage...

We have a grand plan that we are going to eat healthy all week because we want to feel good. We are all set to go; the freezer is stocked, lunches are made, breakfast is prepared the night before, we know what is for dinner, and we have our snacks all planned out...

The first couple of days went great. Then something happens that pisses us off, and we deal with that stress the way we usually do – a whole packet of biscuits / a bottle of wine / a few cans of beer because we 'need' to destress.

Or if you make it to Friday, you celebrate the end of the week with a few drinks and a takeaway (this bit isn't the problem). You wake up feeling a bit shit on Saturday morning, so instead of returning to the plan, you hit the shop for a fry-up with a tonne of toast. Because of the alcohol and salty food the night before, you crave all the salty, sweet and greasy food you can get your hands on. Then decide to have a few more drinks,

Sunday becomes a repeat of Saturday, and you can't face getting the food shop and preparation done for next week.

You are off plan, back to old habits.

At any point through that weekend, you had choices to make; often, instead of thinking further ahead and keeping a goal in mind, we go for instant gratification. If we are stressed, sad, bored, angry or don't want to seem dull, we make rash decisions with an 'I don't care' or 'fuck it' attitude.

The self-sabotage didn't happen at the takeaway and drink on Friday night; it was what happened after. I go into this more in Rule #8, but your decisions need to be around what makes you feel happy in your mind and body. If you sat and really enjoyed the food and drink and didn't feel guilty about it after, that is not self-sabotage.

Self-sabotage is when you are riddled with guilt and lousy feeling, asking yourself, 'Why did I do that?' and then repeating the sabotaging behaviours.

Self-sabotage can also happen when you are not making time for yourself. You put everyone else in front of you when it comes to self-care.

Another thing is not seeking medical advice when something in your body isn't right. If your car wasn't working right, you would go straight to the garage to check it out. Your body is a beautifully crafted machine that needs to be taken care of.

Physical health, mental health, soul health... These can't be ignored. Ignoring them is self-sabotage.

It is so much easier when it's not your fault when you can blame someone else for the downward spiral; partner, kids, a boss or a client putting on demands of you, or thinking it will get better in time...

I have some bad news for you... It won't get better, and it's your fault. You are responsible for and in control of your decisions and the support you seek. If you don't ask, you won't get it.

You say you want to be better, so you need to stop giving yourself excuses. You say you want to look better so that you feel better so that you will be more confident and happier. You say you want to find love, but it seems you don't even love yourself...

Have a think about these questions:

Do you ever prioritise yourself?
Do you make snap decisions without thinking about your end goal?
Do you eat for health?
Do you exercise or do activities that keep you healthy and happy?
Do you have hobbies or interests that entertain you?
Are you learning new things daily to develop yourself to be even more exceptional?

If the honest answer to any of these questions is no (which includes answers of hesitation, sometimes or not really), then you need to ask yourself why? If you have taken time through the previous chapters to work out who you are and thought about your dreams and goals, then you want to keep these at the front of your mind; stop telling yourself it is okay; you will start tomorrow or whatever your excuse is.

'I'm not worth it ', 'I don't deserve this', and 'I'm not good enough' are just a few of the things you might be telling yourself.

We might not say these out loud or to anyone else, but we sure as hell are running these scripts inside, and we need to stop. I know this because I have been guilty, too, and I still need to pull myself in to check at times. Marketing companies want us to feel like we are not worthy. When we feel worthy, we stop buying crap that we don't need.

No fizzy drink makes you more fun; no sanitary product makes you want to go skydiving. No car makes you sophisticated, and no washing powder makes you a better parent.

These constant doubts hold us back from success and happiness and cushion us from failure. Brené Brown discusses this in her Power of Vulnerability book, it is easier to prepare yourself for disappointment so it doesn't feel as bad when it happens, but the problem is we miss out on the opportunity of feeling joy. It isn't possible to numb the negative emotions. All emotions get numbed - this is not good. The good news is that the more open we are to allow ourselves to experience bad or negative emotions, the better we get at dealing with them. We become more resilient and realise that sometimes shit things happen, and we can get up and move on.

This then brings me to think about how we speak to ourselves. Have you ever stopped to take notice of that voice inside your head? I would put money on the fact that (unless you have worked on this before) that person is not very nice to you often.

It puts you down, ridicules you, and creates self-doubt. I used to refer to mine as the 'sergeant major' until I demoted her. When I was at the gym, to get me moving more or lifting heavier, I would call myself a 'fat, lazy bitch' to motivate myself. I was neither fat nor lazy.

When you think about the things you say to yourself, do you ever speak like that to any of your friends? Or had a friend talk to you like that? My money would be on no. If the conversation was like that, I don't know that you would be friends for long. If you have friends that speak to you like that, consider why you are friends with them. If it is to keep you in your place, I would ask you to consider not spending much time with those 'friends' anymore.

So, assuming you don't communicate with others, why do you speak to yourself like that and let yourself get away with it? Sometimes it's a lack of self-awareness, and as I have mentioned earlier, you don't know what you don't know, but we are now looking at bringing attention to that self-awareness.

If you read that last part thinking, 'Jen, I know that I am good enough and deserve the best; I positively speak to

myself....' If you are already achieving everything that you want to achieve, you look and feel fabulous and are delighted with what you see when you look in the mirror – your external appearance as well as your internal self then fantastic, keep doing what you are doing, you are there, you are on the right track and self-sabotage isn't something you need to worry about. Skip to the next chapter.
For the rest of us...

Other than that voice inside your head, people around you might question you, doubting your abilities. My questions to you are; why do you listen? Why do you keep them around? Why are you letting them feed your own self-doubt and self-sabotage? If it's family members that you can't really get away from, you need to get better at allowing their comments to wash over you.

We want to have a network of people with a positive energy that inspires and motivates us and makes us want to be better people and believe in ourselves, particularly when we struggle to believe in ourselves.

Where possible, we want to spend less time with people who bring us down, drain our energy and validate our self-sabotage. The most common reason others try to pull us back is that if we are doing well and are happy, they feel guilty or insecure that they are not doing it for themselves. For some, pulling someone down is easier than raising themselves to a higher level. We don't know what is going on in their world or head.
The room doesn't get brighter, blowing out someone else's candle.

Our emotional health is essential to look after, as is our physical health. The 2 go hand in hand.

How is your skin looking?
Are your eyes bright and sparkling?
Is your hair strong and shiny?

Are your nails and nail beds looking healthy? Are you suffering from any gut health or digestive issues?

When you have skin breakouts and conditions (like acne, eczema and psoriasis), dull eyes, bloodshot eyes, and your hair and weak nails are all tell-tale signs that you are not looking after yourself well. You need to look at what you are eating and if you are drinking enough of and the right kind of fluids, but also you need to be considering how much stress you are under and the quality of your sleep.

When you look in the mirror, are you a shape and size you are happy with? (this is not comparing yourself with some airbrushed magazine cover image).

How are your moods from day to day, even morning to evening?

What about your energy levels and motivation?

Again, all of these can be signs that we are doing things daily that suggest we are not taking care of ourselves (inside and out). Daily self-sabotage is at its base level when we don't eat the right foods, get enough sleep, and/or beneficially deal with stress.

If this is the case, I would like to bring you back to questions such as:

Why are you not taking better care of yourself?
What is so important that your health and well-being are not a priority?
Why is it that when you start working towards a goal and reach a level of success, you hit a wall and stop?
Why do you not just keep going, get to the wall and climb over?

What makes you think this is it; this is the best I can have?

Tiredness and stress significantly affect decision-making and can be the root cause of some self-sabotaging behaviours. How often do you make crap food choices because you can't be bothered, you are having a shit day, or everyone else is eating cake/drinking wine?

So, we have addressed some of the different levels and streams of self-sabotage; just because there is a label for it does not mean it's okay. But, now we know what it is, we have something to work with.

The thing with this self-sabotage (or any belief about yourself) is that when you believe that it's something you do, you are more inclined to use it as an excuse (sometimes even without realising you are). You run the line in your head, 'I self-sabotage everything I do. That's just me – here you are giving yourself a label just like the labels we talked about in Chapter 2; you are not your label. This is a behaviour that you do rather than something that you are... Think of that as the Law of

Attraction the wrong way round; instead of putting out optimistic hopes and desires to get positivity back, you are putting out adverse decisions and excuses that bring back negative actions and situations.

So how do we regain control and start moving in the right direction? A way to get past this and reverse this negative law of attraction is to first recognise when you are self-sabotaging (self-awareness); this means looking out for patterns in your behaviour and results. If you want to change the pattern, you must break the habit. Self-sabotage can feel like a brick wall we hit when you find the wall, climb it, dig through it, get around it, make it crumble, and beat it. Don't let it beat you.

To help you break the pattern, work through the questions in this next exercise. You need to answer the questions honestly. You are the only one that knows this stuff, and understanding where you are coming from and what you allow to get in your way will enable you to break your habits.

Exercise

What is it that stops you from sticking with your goal?
What do you believe about yourself stops you from staying on track? (what doubts about yourself do you have?)
What is it about the action that you don't want to do? (Is there a particular part you don't want to do?)
Why is it okay to not stick to the plan?
Where is that coming from? What is that voice inside your head telling you?
Why do you think this challenge you avoid can't take you to a place of better happiness?
If you have success, what does that mean to you? How will things be different / better for you?

These questions should help you identify what is holding you back. When you have a better understanding of what it is that holds you back, you can then ask yourself

3 simple questions;
COULD I let this feeling go?
Would I let this go?
When will I let this go?

Go back and look at your values list from Chapter 2. Applying them to why you want to achieve your goals can make it easier to stop giving yourself excuses.

If you resist this exercise, we can look at it from a different angle...

Where will you be in 6 months if you keep self-sabotaging? Review the last 6 months to get an idea – are you heavier? Even less fit? Still in the same job? Unhappier?

How often, at the end of the day, do you wish you had just got up and gone to the gym in the morning?

How demotivated do you feel when you put your work clothes on, and they feel a bit tighter instead of looser?

How much more fun would be playing with the kids be if you feel energised and not stressed, exhausted and run down?

How do you feel on your commute to work to that job that you absolutely hate?

How much better would it be if that was your trigger that stopped you and said:

Fuck this; I don't want to feel like crap today/tomorrow / anymore? I want to feel the best I can all day, every day.

I want to look good & feel good. I don't want to hate myself anymore...

How pissed off with yourself do you need to get before you take action?

'I will when I am ready...'

How do you know when you are ready? What is it you are going to be prepared for?

"It's a terrible thing, I think, to wait until you're ready. I have this feeling now that no one is ever ready to do anything. There is almost no such thing as ready. There is only now. And you may as well do it now. Generally speaking, now is as good a time as any." Dr House (Hugh Laurie) – How good was that TV show?!

Why do you need to be ready? What does ready look like to you? Will you ever be ready? Or are you using it to stall because you are afraid? This chapter is full of thought-provoking questions; all of them are useful for you to consider and acknowledge the answers so you can progress (you don't know what you don't know).

Imagine how it would feel to be sitting with a friend enjoying a coffee and cake guilt free rather than inhaling it down with your head in the fridge door so no one sees you? Or how much better it will be when you say no to invitations to things you don't want to go to because you have committed yourself to do something you want to do for yourself... And sometimes that is just doing nothing (you are allowed to do nothing).
To be successful, you have to be in a risk-taking mindset; to be in a risk-taking mindset, you need not be in a self-sabotage mindset. You need to be prepared to do something different to get a positive change. How has doing what you have always done gone for you so far?

So, risks... Actually, I wouldn't say I like that word; let's call them challenges (this is also my go-to word for problems)... risk sounds a bit scary, a bit risky. Risk assessments are looking for danger, and we are not looking for danger. We are looking for those little challenges that in our head seem a bit uncomfortable, maybe unfamiliar; we have no idea how it will turn out. If we think back to all the other challenges we have overcome and turned out well (or not as bad as we imagined – does anything turn out as bad as we imagined?)... Those are the challenges we want to take to help us overcome our self-sabotage.

I am all too familiar with what happens when we start thinking about the challenge. Our imagination takes control, every 'what if' scenario runs through our head, and before we know it, an entirely catastrophic soap opera scene is running in our head. This is not real; this is our imagination (usually fuelled by the TV, social media and movies we watch) triggering to 'protect' you.

Let's take a step back for a moment and look at this from a different angle.

What is the real situation that you are facing?
What would you tell them to do if this was your friend's situation?
How would you reassure them that they will be okay?
What advice would you give them to move forward?

Example 1

Our Mission: To look and feel great at the beach on holiday.

Our Plan: To eat well and get to the gym daily.

Our Self-Sabotage: 'I have been good all week, and I deserve a treat' – that treat can end up being a whole weekend binge because the weeks 'being perfect' was way too restricting, but it's okay; I will start again on Monday. Or something upsetting or stressful happens, and you need to numb the pain with your comfort foods.

Risk: Understand that the 'go hard or go home' 'all or nothing' methods are a set-up to fail. Too much restriction cannot be sustained, and you will make yourself even less happy than before, especially if you feel deprived. Accept small sustainable lifestyle changes, which will mean slower results, but you can maintain them. The most significant risk here is acceptance of the beautiful being that you are right now and that change can't happen overnight.

Example 2

Our Mission: To be in a happy, perfect, secure relationship with our ideal mate.

Our Plan: Have them spot us somewhere, approach us, put in all the groundwork, declare undying love for us and live happily ever after.

Our Self-Sabotage: Waiting for someone else to approach us, why do they need to be the ones to show all the vulnerability? Or set up an online dating profile, date everyone and anyone that asks, then accept the one that sticks around even if they are not the right one for you. Or set up an online dating profile and never connect or date anyone. Or sit in your house complaining (even silently in your own mind) that no one ever asks you out. Or be so guarded that you deflect anyone who dares look at you while declaring that there is no one out there and poor you will be alone forever, so you might as well get the cats in now.

Risk: Firstly, falling in love with yourself, your flaws, and every part of you. This will become easier when you have your values lists and know who you are and what you want and need to allow values with another to fall in line (this doesn't mean that they need to have an exact match list, but they need to complement and balance each other). Speak to strangers! A smile, a hello, or a genuine compliment is a great way to engage in conversation. If they smile and say thanks or look awkward, you can step away unhurt, unembarrassed – you were just being pleasant and genuine. Best case, they engage in conversation, and you get a better idea of who they are. Be prepared to put yourself out there and potentially be rejected with the caveat that if you know and understand your values, rejection isn't rejection; it is a misalignment of values. The most significant risk here is accepting and loving yourself first; without that, there won't be a match.

These are a couple of examples where initially, you think the risk will be significant, but when you step back and break it down, it is not as overwhelming as you first thought. Let go of the big end goal and focus on that next step. Removing the big agenda takes away the big failure fears.

So, stop beating yourself up just because you have made mistakes in the past or because you are not exactly where you would like to be. You are worth the effort, deserve it, and are good enough. Live in the moment – not in the past because it's gone and can't be changed, and the future, it's still to happen, and it can be however you want it to be.

It's time to fall in love with yourself, show respect, and start trusting yourself to give things a go.

There comes a time in everyone's life when they need to stop bullshitting themselves. Eventually, You will get pissed off with yourself and realise it's time to take responsibility, control, and prioritise yourself. At the end of the day, it is down to you to make the change and be happy.

Exercise
Write a list of the 5 things you hate about yourself.
Then list the 5 things you love or are most happy with.
Using the 5 things you are most happy with, look at how you can use them to your advantage to change the things you are least satisfied with.
Please write it down. Make a plan. Start working on it.
The time to stop self-sabotaging is over.

Action

- Breathe
- Accept responsibility for your actions
- Be honest with yourself, always
- Give yourself a break
- Meditate
- Be around the right people
- Find a mentor(s) or coach(es) for all areas of your life, these don't necessarily need to cost money although in some areas of expertise it may be worth it.
- Call yourself out and analyse the risk (the real risk)
- Start with small risks that you know are not the end of the world either way to build some confidence and reassure you that your world won't end if things don't work out how you hope.

Rule #4

Breathe

All this talk of self-sabotage and risk-taking (or avoidance of risk-taking) brings us to the lovely world of stress.

The dictionary definition of stress:
Noun – a state of mental or emotional strain or tension resulting from adverse or demanding circumstances.
Verb – cause mental or emotional strain or tension

On the surface, I come across as someone who doesn't really let things bother me, My mood is neither up nor down when faced with challenges, and I pretty much take things in my stride...

What I discovered in the years post my divorce was that I was someone who did not deal with emotional stress very well. Until that point in my life, the emotional stress I had to deal with was death - and I didn't deal with it; I managed it. I was lacking in emotional intelligence.

I had always been referred to as a 'strong person' who could deal with anything, and at that point, I felt that was what was expected and rolled with it.

What I realised was I was very good at numbing my emotions. When I spoke of my marriage ending, I regularly stated that I wasn't bothered, it was the right thing to happen for both of us (which logically it was), or I was too busy to be worrying about it – an active mind doesn't have time to be sad.

My head was firmly buried in the sand; I was numbing my pain with busyness, food, drink and 'fun'. I could not be alone and not idle – now I realise these should have been loud alarm bells ringing, and they probably were; I just chose not to hear them. I managed to ignore and numb the pain for about 18 months before I had to deal with things, and I started going for NLP therapy.

It wasn't until early 2013 that the stress (that I had been burying) bit me on the ass and completely floored me. I was ultimately out of action for 2 whole weeks (getting out of bed to get to the bathroom took all my effort), and it took nearly another 18 months to fully recover. Had the doctor's not scared the shit out of me by mentioning the possibility of cancer-like symptoms, I would have possibly ignored them and gone back to my old ways.

Since the first edition of this book, I also learned the dangers around suppressed emotions, intense physical stress from doing too much exercise, and not having an appropriate recovery regime and how damaging sleep deprivation is. In March 2017, I was diagnosed with Crohn's. Everything I learned on that journey is for another book. But I now know your body will eventually stop you if you don't listen to the signals it sends.

Stress can be your best friend at times and also your worst enemy. We need the stress responses to wake up each morning, hit our deadlines and survival... Back in the day, it saved us from being eaten by wild animals. The wild animal killing us today comes from our hectic 24/7 lifestyles, overworking and not taking enough care of ourselves and our well-being.

Sleep deprivation occurs with only 2 consecutive nights of less than 7 hours of sleep (how many hours a night do you get??), and the research shows this causes inflammation in the body which can be linked to some illnesses, including obesity, cancer, inflammatory bowel disease, depression, and anxiety among others. Sleep deprivation is probably one of the most common stresses that the clients I have worked with have; for some, it is getting to sleep, others being restless or not staying asleep all night, and others waking up really early.

Common symptoms of stress (this list is not exhaustive):
- Anxiety,
- Depression
- Overwhelm
- Confusion
- Panic (including attacks)
- Lack of ability to chill out
- Burnout (losing your mojo)
- Low or no libido
- Constant unexplained headaches
- Nausea
- Binge eating /no appetite
- Skin breakouts such as eczema, acne, and psoriasis
- Bad sleeping patterns (not sleeping enough, too much or at sporadic times)
- Muscle tension (how is your back, neck and shoulders?)
- Mood swings or a bad temper
- Low immune system (always getting a cold, chest infections etc.)
- Inflammation in the body (eczema, psoriasis, asthma, cancer, IBD, IBS etc.)

**Please know that some of these symptoms may be related to an underlying illness or side effects to medication (including the contraceptive pill) or for females connected to your monthly cycle, so always get checked out by a health professional and track your moods and feelings for a couple of months to see if there is any pattern developing.

I imagine many of us have experienced at least one or two of those symptoms in our lifetime, sometimes relating to stress even if we haven't particularly identified the link; sometimes, it has been an illness which may (or may not) have been brought on by stress, although it's now known that stress weakens the immune system.

Some of the more common causes of stress I have come across with myself and my clients (again, this list is not exhaustive, what is stressful to one person could be complete chill out to another):

- Working too much, not taking time to relax.
- Not breathing properly
- Not getting enough good quality sleep
- Not taking time to play/be creative
- Too much intense exercise without sufficient recovery time
- Drinking stimulants (coffee, energy drinks, alcohol).
- Overthinking or not letting things go.
- Numbing your emotions / bottling everything up inside.
- Drug use (prescription and non)

Some symptoms include 'which came first, the chicken or the egg'. For example, I suffer from eczema, which I have done since I was 18 months old. Sometimes a breakout will be caused by food intolerance (usually dairy, wheat, and sugar), but sometimes, I could eat those things and not have a breakout...

Sometimes I didn't eat any of those things, and my skin would still flare up.

It drove me mad until I went on a yoga breathing course where we spent 3 hours learning how to breathe correctly (you would be surprised how many different ways of breathing there are). On the day of the course, I had an eczema breakout, the following morning, I woke up, and my skin was pretty clear. Whenever I start to get a breakout, I take time out and focus on my breathing, and the symptoms reduce.

As I said before, I am not a healthcare professional who can prescribe treatments, but this works for me for this specific stress. When I focus on my breathing, it reduces stress in my body, reducing the symptoms. My thought process of 'if I breathe properly, I can have bread' motivates me.

Sleep and meditation have also been hugely beneficial in my healing process of Crohn's.

You may have noticed in the Actions at the end of each chapter Breathe is one of the actions. It is also something I regularly teach clients and consistently get good feedback about how much better people feel, just taking a few minutes each day to focus on their breath.

Over the last few years, I have also done extensive work using NLP, coaching, Yoga, EFT, Reiki, and hypnotherapy to deal with the more significant stresses. For some people, that type of treatment is sufficient; for others, they may need more focused and more direct therapy and coaching.

As I mentioned before, some stress is good for you – it's the hormone that wakes you up in the morning, creates the health benefits of exercise, lets you feel the excitement, makes you aware of the danger, and sometimes a bit of pressure to meet a deadline is just what you need to stay focused – getting a report (or in my case a book) written on time, getting the kids out the door to school/activities on time...

We have created a world where we are accessible 24/7 and plugged in constantly... Technology can make life easier and get things done faster, but on the other side of that, we have created a monster for ourselves. We have set the conditions of being unable to switch off; we respond to emails or messages even when we are supposed to be on a day off or family time.

Who completely unplugs the way we used to when you go on holiday? Then we feel guilty about losing control of our mental health and happiness if we try to switch off. It is up to us to take responsibility to set the boundaries of when we will reply. My auto responder tells the person making contact that I don't work 24/7, neither should they, and I will get back to them as soon as possible.

A popular trend seems to be emerging for people to wear their stress and exhaustion as a badge of honour/status symbol to prove how hardworking they are... 'I was up till 3 am working' 'I live on 4 hours sleep a night' 'You can rest when you are dead' or 'Work hard, play hard', 'Everyone needs me, and I just can't ignore them' or 'I just don't have time'.

This mindset and action are not suitable for your stress levels or health; it will only contribute to ill health or premature death (yes, that is drastic). It is almost seen as shameful if you take time out to do fun and relaxing stuff without your phone being glued to your hand... We need to change that way of thinking and make work time focused on work and rest time concentrate on rest.

For us women, if we are not doing it all (career, family, fun) and looking fabulous (perfect hair, makeup, clothes, body) while doing it... well, we should be ashamed of ourselves for letting it slip... Kiss. My. Ass. We are real, we are human, we are amazing, and we are not Stepford Wives. I see so many men out there busting their asses, expected to deliver society's high demands, constantly under pressure and not talking about it; they have to 'man up'... I am so delighted that so many reached out to me asking for a gender-neutral edition of this book to be written and also the rise in men talking about their mental health.

Suicide rates are on the increase, which is terrifying. There is so much self-inflicted pressure to keep up and have the best house/car / latest tech that no one is having any fun. It needs to stop. Fun needs to come much higher on the priority list, and we need to remember the fun that didn't mean taking out a second mortgage.

Who defines this image that so many are trying to be anyway? We can blame the media or celebrities, marketing companies or TV, but ultimately, we must take responsibility for the pressure we put on ourselves. We have the power to say no. Be confident about who you are, what you look like and what you have. Having all that 'stuff' and looking 'perfect' doesn't make us happy, even if we have the cash to afford it.

How often do you take some downtime and feel guilty about it?

Maybe all you are doing is sitting on the sofa having tea or coffee, and in your head, all you can think about is the emails, housework, the next goal on the list or whatever is not allowing you to sit in peace because everything feels like a priority.

I would get agitated in the past if I sat down to chill... but now I have become a master at it. There are still times when I sit down, and I remember the washing needs to be hung, the dishwasher needs to be emptied, and sometimes I leave it and get it later. It has taken me a good couple of years and a chronic disease diagnosis to get me to where I stopped. I urge you not to wait for a chronic disease to slow you down. It's shite.

So, you must let go of this need to be superhuman and always perfect. It's exhausting and slowly killing us. So what if the house is untidy for another 15 minutes, so

what if someone emailed you expecting a reply?! What happens if you wait 15mins?
Nothing!

It can be easy to blame external sources for your stresses; your boss is demanding deadlines are met, your partner wants time with you, the kids need help with their homework, extended family and friends wish some of your time, work, the government, the weather, the bus/train driver, the shopkeeper... It could be anyone and everyone else's fault because they all want a piece of you.

We have to take responsibility for ourselves, our actions, and our boundaries.

It's your fault... (harsh but true, you must take responsibility). You are the one that keeps saying yes to everyone else and no to yourself.

This doesn't mean that you think of yourself as a failure. This is about you taking responsibility and control of your own happiness. Say 'yes' to more things that make you happy and 'no' to things that don't make you happy or drain your time and energy. And ask for help. It is easier to play the blame game, but we are trying to do too much and always show up as perfect. You are human, which means you are not perfect, your environment is not perfect, and life isn't perfect, so you need to let go of that stress and be imperfect.

Take a breath; yes, I said to be imperfect; this comes from a 'perfectionist in recovery. I am not suggesting that you stop giving a shit, but take the pressure off a bit, give your best effort each time, and know that is all anyone should expect of you.

You are in control of yourself and your life, and you can take yourself out of a situation or change your reaction to it at any time. First, you need to breathe and assess the situation. My favourite questions to ask myself and get my clients to ask themselves when they find themselves in a stressful situation are:
Is this okay?

And;
What is the best way I can deal with this situation right now?

It is up to you to say 'no' when it means you are putting yourself out by saying yes. It is up to you to switch off your phone/laptop and not be available on demand. There was no signal, or the battery died are great excuses if you feel like you need one. And it's up to you to detach yourself emotionally from a situation you have no control over.

If your boss keeps loading work onto you, it's because you are so freaking awesome and they trust you, but it's also because you keep saying 'yes'. You need to let them know that you are a fantastic human being, but now you are sorting your shit and not pretending to be superhuman anymore... You, your happiness and your health are way more important.

If the kids want to be part of every after-school club and activity, it is up to you to decide what and where you can reasonably get to or team up with other parents to take turns to take them. One of my friends has a strict rule that after 8pm, it is her time, and her kids have learned that they need to respect that or deal with the consequences of a really grumpy mum – there is some flexibility there when it is, required but it works really well for them as a family to have set those boundaries and respect. This is equally important in relationships to have a couple time and individual time.

There may be people in your life constantly demanding time and support from you, and you never seem to get any in return.
Are you there as the problem solver? Do you look for their problems, solve the problems, give advice, hold their hands, love them, care for them, be their rock, pick up after them – you get a real sense of being needed, but when it starts to be taken for granted, and you are getting stressed and emotionally drained, you need to learn to say no and find your own support...

The people around you are not mind readers, not your boss, kids, partner, friends or anyone else. You need to speak up, ask for help, and learn to stop fixing everything. They need to learn for themselves, and they will manage. You are there to be a leader, to guide them to solving their own stuff, making them their own leader; believe me, they will thank you for it later when they find themselves not getting bogged down with everyone else's crap.

The government... What can we say... They do their thing; we need to do ours. Maybe one of you has aspirations to lead the country... What is it that is stopping you from going for it?

The weather... As Billy Connelly famously said, 'There is no such thing as bad weather, only the wrong clothes'. For those of us in the UK, it rains (a lot). This is nothing new, some summers are good, and some are bad... There really is nothing you can do except buy really cool all-weather gear and an umbrella.

When dealing with other people, it is worth remembering that everyone has their own problems and shit to deal with. I don't want to burst your bubble, but other people are so wrapped up in their own issues that you won't be their highest priority, just like they shouldn't be yours. If people are rude, in a bad mood or give lousy service, take a moment to consider that they might have something else going on or that they haven't found this book to help them feel better (you can always pass on the book or link to the book for them to buy – shameless plug).

If you have ever done anything a bit mad and out of character or afterwards thought, 'What the hell made me react like that / do that / say that?' it has likely been something else completely stressing you out, blocking your brain and clear thought processes. You know, things like sending a text/email in haste, throwing stuff out the window, throwing a drink over someone, saying something you don't mean, standing up and forgetting instantly what you were going to do, buying the wrong milk, finding your keys in the fridge, impulse shopping, binge eating, generally making silly mistakes. It's fair to say that we have all, at some point, at least once, reacted to something like that list.
Well, that is stress taking control of you instead of you taking control of the situation.

Brilliant, I can hear you say, but what can we do to start to take better control?

Exercise

There are many ways to combat stress, depending on where your source comes from, and everyone has different success with different things. Try these different techniques to see which ones are most effective and best suited for you. What is suitable for one is only sometimes good for another.

Breathe. The best thing about this exercise is you can do it anywhere and anytime.

- Think about how you breathe right now. Just notice it. Be aware. Are you just breathing into the top part of your chest? (it's common to breathe into the top part of our chest when we are not thinking about it, are really busy or are stressed).
- Start to slow your breathing down. Try to fill your lungs, let your rib cage move out the way, and let your belly relax, then slowly let that breath out as fully as possible.
- Do this for 3 full breaths. When breathing out fully, you clear the stale air at the bottom of the lungs.
- Start counting your breath; count how long it takes you to fully breathe in and how long it takes you to fully breathe out. Once you have your number (most people are between 3 & 8, but there is no goal), match your inhale and exhale to be the exact count, and make it as smooth as possible.

Do this at least every morning and evening (more often if you can), for about 5 minutes when you wake up when you are sitting in traffic, on your commute to work, after a difficult phone call or meeting (before if you know you are going into a difficult call or meeting), while you are on the toilet, waiting for the kettle to boil, while you are reading...

That exercise is a form of meditation; taking your mind away from everything else and focusing on your breath settles, calms and clears your mind, allowing you to better deal with everything else. You may find that you get better ideas, do better work and are more creative.

Adjusting your physiology & posture (how you are sitting or standing) will significantly impact your mood and stress. Think about how you sit or stand when feeling down, low in confidence, and sad... Your head is down, shoulders rounded, hunched forward. It is challenging to breathe correctly in this position. How do you sit at your desk, in the car, huddled under your umbrella, or when you are on your phone???

Then think about how you sit or stand when you feel good, chest lifted, shoulders back and open, up straight – You need to do more of this right here and make a habit of it.

- Sit or stand up straight (the more you can stand, the better; sitting is the new smoking because of its negative impact on our health).
- Relax your shoulders away from your ears.
- Tuck your chin slightly so your ears are over your shoulders and your neck is nice and long.
- Draw your shoulders back so the shoulder blades sit comfortably on your rib cage; this should open your chest, allowing you to breathe easier.
- Lift and narrow your waist without allowing the ribs to lift up; this should make you feel taller and narrower – this should be a light engagement,

not a full contraction, so you can't breathe smoothly.

- Hold your pelvis in a neutral position (hip bones and pubic bone are in alignment with each other – use the heel of your hands on your hip bones and middle fingers in towards your pubic bone to check the alignment)
- Whether seated or standing, place your feet and knees hip-width apart (roughly a fist distance between your knees) and try to evenly distribute your weight between the right and left.
- Breathe; your body should feel comfortable and relaxed in this position with no tension or pressure being held anywhere other than your core to support your posture.

Unplug from technology. Everyone finds this challenging, particularly at first if you reach for your phone every 2 mins. Statistics for 2018 are we look at our phones on average 70 times a day. That is underestimated. Get an app that will tell you that information, plus how long you have spent on your phone. Even on a day when I think I have hardly been on my phone because I have been busy, I still hit at least 2hrs screen time!

Unplugging from your tech is essential, and once you have done it a couple of times and notice how much better you feel, you will want to make sure you are fitting in sometime every day.

- Have 1 day a week that you can go as technology free as possible, or even have set times of the day you do and don't use it (like meal times, family time, down time). This includes phones, tablets, laptops, PCs, TV, Alexa, and any tech!!

- Read real books instead of social media.
- Go for walks (fresh air is fantastic for stress reduction)
- Go on a road trip
- Meet friends or family for coffee, lunch, or dinner.
- Connecting with nature and/or animals and/ or people in real life is a fantastic stress reliever and fun (when you are with the right people).
- Take yourself out of your 24/7 contact world, and set new rules to use technology less daily.

Don't re-live drama. When someone or something upsets you, acknowledge your feelings and move on. If you keep thinking and talking about what happened, you keep the emotions running, 'You won't believe what he/she just said/did to me... blah, blah, blah'. The more you relive, the worse the emotion feels because you keep topping it up and stay in that negative state longer. Let the past be the past. This includes road rage and breathing through it.

When you feel a negative thought or emotion coming up, acknowledge the emotion and why you are experiencing it (we are allowed to be sad or angry, we want to avoid wallowing in it). Then if it is appropriate to move on from that emotion, do something to distract yourself. An emotion only lasts a few seconds; our mind and imagination keep it going and reliving it.

Write a gratitude journal. Research has shown that people who write and practice gratitude are happier and less stressed. The more you focus on the good things in your life that you are thankful for, the less stressed and more positive your thoughts stay. Get a special journal to write in (my I Am | Positively Grateful journal is available on Amazon) with a good pen – and write in it. I have had notebooks that I deemed 'too pretty to write in', and I was scared to make a mistake, so I didn't use them. It's just paper, make mistakes, and nothing terrible will happen.

- Every day in the morning, write 3 things you are grateful for and why you are thankful for it
- At the end of the day, another 3 items, remember your why.
- If you have more than 3, keep writing. Don't hold back.

Doing exercise in some form of physical activity produces good stress, which boosts your metabolism, grows muscles, improves bone density, improves sleep, reduces blood pressure and improves general health, but if overdone, it will create bad stress, which is detrimental to all the benefits it can make.
If you are mentally exhausted, exercise is a perfect way to clear your head and let you feel re-energised because the brain uses a different part for thinking than it does moving and when you are concentrating on your exercises, you don't think about anything else (just like when you are focusing on breathing).

Exercise becomes a problem when you work out at too high an intensity for too long, go back for another session too soon without proper recovery, or exercise without enough sleep/food/hydration or too many stimulants. If you go into a session feeling weak and lethargic, you will do more harm than good. Gentle exercises like Yoga, Pilates or walking are best when you feel that way but also feel like you really need to do something. Always listen to your body; if you start a workout and feel worse, stop doing it.

If you are unsure, ask for help and get booked with a personal trainer that advocates a good quality diet and rest times; if they operate a 'beast mode' or 'go hard or go home' policy, I recommend avoiding them. Watch how the trainers are with their clients in the gym, speak with the clients and other gym members about their experiences, and meet to talk with the trainer before you sign up; make sure you like them, and you feel a good vibe from them. Look at their social media pages. Are they all about their clients and their results, or is it all pictures of them flexing in the gym? That will give you a good indication of where their priorities lie.

Smile. This is a fantastic stress reliever; even if you don't want to smile, do it anyway. It signals to your brain that something is making you happy, and all the right delighted chemicals start to release, lifting your mood. If your face genuinely does not want the corners of your mouth to turn up, hold a pencil or pen across your teeth so that the ends of the pencil are forcing the edges of your mouth out wide (just like a smile). It works ☺. Even increasing the smile to laughter is even more effective.

Action

- Breathe
- Accept responsibility for your actions
- Be honest with yourself, always
- Give yourself a break
- Meditate
- Reduce your use of technology
- If you have a work phone, switch it off when you are not on duty
- Ask for help
- Eat good healthy food
- Practice gratitude
- Exercise or move regularly
- Don't feel guilty for doing things that are fun
- Smile / laugh
- Give yourself a break
- Breathe

Rule #5

Find your flow

of

Masculine and Feminine
energy

In life, we have many different relationships, and every single one has a different connection and purpose. Family, friends, lovers, work colleagues, bosses, people who serve us, people we serve, people we meet in passing and, of course, ourselves.

There is a variety of them, and we will connect to each differently and for various reasons.

In this rule, I am talking to you about your energy (as in a vibe or flow rather than how energetic and enthusiastic you feel); this can be a lot to take in, but please stay with me while I explain.

Every single one of us has masculine and feminine energy – remember that this has nothing to do with your physical appearance or sexual organs, or sexual preference. It concerns your energy and flow, how you think and feel and react to things, particularly when you feel stressed or under 'threat'. Who you are at work can also be different to who you are at home and who you come into contact with.

Masculine energy: driven, focused, analytical, decisive, leader, deliver, fixer, linear, logical, has a need to complete or finish a task, competitive, want to sort things out to make people happy, stop at nothing – think athletes in competition

Feminine energy: emotional, likes to talk and feel feelings, intuitive, goes with the flow, doesn't like to make decisions, breezy, receivers, creative, multi-taskers, can have lots of unfinished tasks, passionate and like to work with others – think a parent nurturing and comforting their child.

In an ideal world, we would all be in harmony with both and can move between each to react and respond to our situation or other people we are in contact with. Many of us, though, fall more strongly to one than the other to where it feels most comfortable when we feel under pressure.

I default to masculine, like to be in charge, am independent, not good at letting people help me, don't read instructions or ask for directions, and like things to be in order and analytical. God help anyone who tries to tell me who I am or what I want in life; if someone tries to alpha me (particularly if they don't know me), they generally get alpha Jen right back in their face. I will be majorly defensive and protective of myself and the situation. This can be very different, though I will soften if I am around a strong masculine energy that I fully trust.

My mum is oh so feminine, she can be indecisive and likes other people to take charge and look after her, she also wants to offer solutions to all your problems and talk about feelings, and she is so creative, she is a beautiful and talented painter.

Just because these are our default energies, that doesn't mean that we don't have or can't access the opposing side. If I trust someone entirely or am completely exhausted and need someone to take over, I will allow them to take control of a situation. My partner Kris and best friend Grant are those masculine energies that get to be boss (sometimes).

When we used to go on holiday as a family, and even now when my mum and dad go away, my mum books the holiday, sorts all the packing and money, holds the tickets and passports, and knows all the details of where and when to be, all my dad needs to do is turn up and carry the suitcase. She even took control and entirely organised my wedding for me.

Our default is where we feel safe and secure (taking control or giving it to someone else). Stuck in one or other energy can sometimes feel challenging and draining, even when it is your default.

Your surroundings can also affect your energy; if you think of a big city with towering buildings, straight lines, and strong edges, the energy there is very masculine; it's busy, and things get done in that city. People who have strong feminine energy might not feel comfortable there; even being overwhelmed or being there might encourage the masculine side to come out, and they can be inspired there.

On the other hand, going out into the countryside is feminine energy; you are with nature where things are softer and flowing, and the energy is totally different, more laid back, calm and easy. Someone with masculine energy may again feel on edge there, searching for hustle, or they may allow themselves to freely release into their feminine and kick back, enjoying the more relaxed space where they may find their creative side is nurtured.

In an ideal world, we would move freely between the energy appropriate to the situations we find ourselves in. Learning about this and where I operated helped me understand why I was the way I was in each environment and around different people. This has helped me feel more relaxed and given me the skill to move more freely between energies. It can be learned.

So how do you know which you fall to?

When you are feeling stressed out or are out of your comfort zone, have a look at your actions;

How do you react?

When do you feel most comfortable?

What's happening in your world when everything in it feels right?

For those of us who are more masculine energy, you like to be the boss, in control, and independent, and if you have the wrong understanding of being feminine (which I did for a long time), you can feel like you are weak and inadequate (especially asking for help). Be reassured that this is not the case; vulnerability is a beautiful and courageous strength (so I have learned). Asking for help allows others to give us the gift of their skills.

I remember seeing somewhere (I am pretty sure it   was a David Deida book) a quote:

'You must trust that the feminine side of yourself is not stupid, inadequate or weak.'

This stopped me; I had always identified that asking for help or admitting I couldn't do something was a sign of weakness. Being open and creative and allowing other people to make decisions is a robust energy exchange,

AND it can also help release some of the stress we put ourselves under.

For those who lean more towards feminine energy, being confident, taking control of a situation, and becoming a bit more decisive and competitive will not scare people away from you. In fact, taking control, even putting on your brave pants occasionally, is not a bad thing, and it is excellent to boost your confidence as you learn your strengths. You have a lot of nurturing and creativity in your bones, which is fantastic. When you take that forward and do something with it that can impact your life or someone around you, it will have a positive ripple effect.

As humans that want to sort our shit, we need to respect and live both sides of the energy, which will be a learning process but totally worth the effort. If something in the past has happened that has pushed you more strongly into one of those energies, working on believing and trusting yourself is going to be a big part of the process of finding a better flow.

So, how do you become more harmonised?

You have to learn to trust yourself and love yourself. When you trust and love yourself, you may discover strengths you never realised you had. You can soften, ask for and accept help, become vulnerable or be able to stand up for yourself, showing the world you are strong, confident, and independent with your brave pants on.

Start with small steps and small decisions to build up your confidence. If you are reaching out and asking for help, watch the person you are asking respond, you will likely see the joy in them that they have been able to help. I know that when I ask Kris for help, he gets all happy because he feels needed. On the other hand, if you are learning to do things independently, notice the satisfaction of completing a challenge; it will boost your confidence.

There will be people who bring out the opposite in you to allow you that better balance, values will be aligned, and it will work nicely. For the masculine energy folks, there will be people in your life who are as masculine energy, and you trust and allow them to charge and do things for you... Let them help. Or in the opposite; for the feminine energy folks, there will be people who need you to step up and take control of situations and do it... Show yourself and the world that you can be the boss (even when being the boss means letting someone else take charge. Understanding and working with your values in this will be really beneficial.

Once you get your head around the differences within the energies and understand who you are, who other people are and what roles the other people are in your life fill, it lets you know your relationships better.

You will learn how to be with others to bring the best out of them and the best to the situation to make it work.

If you have 2 feminine energies running a business, the creative ideas will be unique, but one of you needs to take control and bring the masculine energy to the table to ensure tasks get completed. Likewise, if you have 2 masculine energies, one of you will have to allow the other to be in charge and take direction. When you move from the more assertive masculine, it will enable you to be more creative.

If you are a parent at home, there will be times that you need to be masculine to get the kids ready and wherever they need to be, and other times that you allow your feminine energy to flow and let them be kids.

If you are in a relationship understanding each other's roles within the relationship can help that work and flow much better. We have a massive social shift where there are no longer tasks that women are supposed to do or tasks men are supposed to do. We all can do all; it's up to us within the household to delegate duties.

Consider where you are on the scale. Are you more one than the other, or are you somewhat harmonised?

It can be easy to be in harmony when things are going well; you will be more aware of a shift when you feel threatened or stressed, and your fight or flight defence system kicks in. Whatever your instincts are, know that's okay; work with your strengths but be mindful of how it impacts the situation. If you are locking heads with someone, or a decision can't be made, something needs to change to improve the situation. Because you are learning and understanding this, you will take responsibility and help make the situation as easy as possible.

Once you know where you sit, think about the relationships you have in your life.

Understanding the balance helps improve your relationships and your contact with others. There will always be people who motivate, inspire, and make you feel amazing, and you look forward to spending time with them, and you leave feeling energised and excited about life. These will likely be the people that harmonise and work well with your energy. Whether they let you be masculine or feminine, it will fit and flow nicely.

At the opposite end of the scale, there will be people you dread seeing. They can bring out negative, insecure and exhausting feelings. These will be the people who challenge your energy. It could be two masculine clashing heads or two feminines where neither will decide about anything or even one masculine and one feminine that can't find the right balance and wind each other up. Sometimes when you are masculine energy all day at work, the last thing you want to do at home is more of the same (or vice versa).

Then there will be other people somewhere in between. Maybe sometimes in harmony, sometimes entirely out of whack. Perhaps you can only deal with each other when you are both in a particular frame of mind...

Understanding this helped me understand others, work better with others and know when to let some things go so certain relationships work better. There will always be people you have to deal with that will challenge you, and there sometimes is no getting around it when there is a clash. You are now empowered with this knowledge and can use it to a positive advantage (but not to manipulate it in a deceptive way).

It would be easy for me to just tell you to spend lots of time with the positive-impacting people and no time with the negative people. That isn't the case in the real world, and it's not necessarily bad. You get to learn, you get stronger, you become more resilient, and you will improve your patience. The good news is that we have learned about ourselves through the last 4 rules, and what we now know about masculine and feminine energy balance, we are better equipped to deal with them. Upskilling all the way.

Energy is one part of people; another is our values which we have looked at back in Rule 1. If you find people draining or forcing you across energy systems that don't work for you, you can look at the values being misaligned for you and work out how to improve the situation for both of you.

For example, if someone is forcing their masculine energy and you feel disrespected when respect is a high value, matching their masculine energy and having a conversation about respect could be an effective way of dealing with the situation. If you matched that masculine energy with feminine energy and started talking about feelings and emotions, you could be met with resistance and a lack of understanding.

It helps with conflict situations when you sit down and listen to each other. When conversing with them to get them to see and understand what and why the situation isn't working for you, you have to be prepared to do the same. 'I hear what you are saying...' (recap what you understand from what you have heard). This allows good communication and ensures that you are both on the same page of understanding. Not being listened to is the most frustrating thing for anyone, no matter where their energy lies.

Regardless of whether or not there is conflict in a relationship, you always have to set boundaries. I always find honesty is the best policy. Some people are utterly blind to the fact that there is even a problem. When there is no conflict in a relationship, having boundaries always allows you to have your own space, and everyone knows where they stand, what you are prepared to do and what is entirely out of the question. A common fault we have is saying 'Yes' to everyone all the time to the point we run ourselves into the ground.

Having this understanding can help you be more adaptable, build better relationships with others and also help you improve and manage the more challenging ones. You are responsible for your actions and reactions, not anyone else's.

NB. Please remember and use this understanding of energy for the greater good of all your relationships and NOT to manipulate or have power over others (I have seen this in action, which isn't pleasant).

The most important relationship you need to have and work on is with yourself. This is the only one you have total control over and the first step to understanding who you are and why you are the way you are.

When we think back over the previous rules, and we are living up to our values, following your dreams and goals, letting go of self-sabotage, dealing with your stress and then including this rule of flow, we can absolutely accept ourselves, making friends with any part of yourself you don't like and actually learn (if you don't already) to love yourself.

When this is in place, you will set the standards of how you expect to be treated because people see how you treat yourself and match that respect. You are the leader of your own life, setting the example to everyone and anyone around you learning from you (and if you ever get the honour to discover the number of people you impact, you will be blown away). We are all teachers to each other, and we are open to learning.

Action

- Breathe
- Accept responsibility for your actions
- Be honest with yourself, always
- Give yourself a break
- Meditate
- Understand your energy balance
- Align it with your values
- Be aware of the balance in relationships with others
- Take responsibility for your own energy

Rule #6

Stop cleaning, start creating

How many times do you find yourself putting things off, stalling, 'I will do it later', 'I will start tomorrow', 'I will start on Monday/next week/1st Jan' snoozing calendar reminders, scrolling through social media mid-task, re-prioritising because the other thing is just so much more interesting, or waiting for the right time?

I have news for you... Now brace yourself...
There is no such time as the right time, and things only happen when YOU take action. Yikes!

The good news is, though, you are not alone in the world of procrastinators; procrastination is something that I talk about a lot with clients; I have asked in my social media groups, 'What do you do when everything feels like a priority?' Every single answer that came back was some procrastination or panic, and I ran away.

If procrastination was an Olympic sport, I would have a good chance of a gold medal. It is always the things that challenge us and push us out of our comfort zone that we are happiest to avoid.

When I was at university, my house must have been the cleanest house on the block. It only took me until my final year of studying to work out that I would have heaps of spare time and a lot less stress if I stopped with the excuses and just got the assignments done. I ended up being that ass hole who was gloating because she had everything ready and handed in as soon as the portal opened while everyone else was starting and panicking.

The first time I needed to do a video link for my programme Warrior Woman Project® it took me about 4 months to actually do it; I had all the excuses, my roots needed to be done, my fringe was too long, I had the wrong top on, my skin wasn't looking great, I forgot, or the laptop was playing up... In the end... 37 seconds of video, I did it and put it online.

The main reason for the delay was I didn't want people to see me, which is stupid because they need to see me. I have excellent courses, books, podcasts, YouTube channel, etc., that help people find balance in life, be better versions of themselves and stop procrastinating...

Often the thing holding us back is fear. Fear of being a failure, being successful, or just being seen. Once you get over yourself and do what needs to be done, you feel pretty damn good and more confident... Proud even.

Procrastination is something we have mastered over the years, and it is also something that infuriates us. When it comes to overcoming procrastination, the questions I get asked the most are:

How do I stop procrastinating?
How do I stop my To Do list from overwhelming me?
How do I get motivated to get stuff done?

Now, I am not about to pass you a get-out-of-jail-free card here; however, sometimes (just sometimes), we need to procrastinate to get the best result out of ourselves. You sometimes need to take a bit of time to get your head clear and make sure that what you are doing is the right thing for you and that you are not just jumping in without thinking about it (4 months for a 37-second video was not an acceptable amount of time). Sometimes that delay can teach us more about who we are and make sure we are in the right place when we do take action. Conversely, taking action and failing can also be the lesson we need to take us to the right place.

One of the challenges around procrastination; how do you know when to hold back and when to take the leap of faith?

We know what it is we should be doing. We know what the answers are. We can feel it in our gut, but we let our ego-chatty mind kick in and throw doubt at our decision-making. This makes decisions challenging... Our choices are always right, even when they don't turn out how we want them to. The job you didn't get, the boy/girl who knocked you back, the outfit that isn't available in your size, the holiday that you didn't go on – none of them were meant for you, and better things will come when the time is right. I don't believe 'what's for you won't go by you'; everything will go by you if you are sitting back and not taking any action because you are 'waiting for the right moment'. In taking action, you get to experience a whole lot more and answer a whole lot faster.

If you often think 'could've, should've, would've,' then you regret the decisions you didn't make (although, by not making a decision, you are still deciding to not take action).

If you find yourself feeling overwhelmed making a decision or if you let fear paralyse you from progressing through life towards those dreams and goals. You need a plan to help you get unstuck.

What do we do when faffing about, delaying decisions, or avoiding responsibility? How do we get over these feelings of being overwhelmed or fearful?

Exercise

Take a deep breath, stop thinking about your goals, and focus on your breath. As soon as you find your mind starts to wander, bring it back to your breath. Spend a few moments here just breathing, allowing your mind to calm and settle.

You can return to your task once you start feeling calmer and more settled. From a distant viewpoint, begin to make a list or look at your To Do list to establish what needs to be done or decided.

What part of the thing is it that you are really avoiding? How about breaking that down more to make it less daunting?
Are there genuine pros and cons to the outcome?

Try to keep focused on the next step rather than the end goal.
The overwhelm often creeps in when the end goal seems too far away.

Keeping in mind the best-case scenario, make a list of all the positive outcomes that will come from completing the task or making the decision, have this list include both the emotional and material positives.
For example, on my task of being creative daily, my positive outcomes include peace, calm, de-stress, vulnerability, business productivity, increased income and learning.

Then I want you to think about what your world will look like when you have completed the task. Add that to your list. Hopefully, you are writing it down to make it more effective, clear and powerful, but if it's a mental note, then take time to think about that too.

Something that I haven't mentioned before is tapping into your imagination. I would like you to imagine the future. Close your eyes and visualise the completed task, jump right to the endpoint where everything is done, and don't think about the journey you may or may not take to get there, and have the focus just on the final goal. Get a clear picture of this in your mind, think about what you would see, hear, and feel, and tap into your senses here; maybe even what you would smell or taste might be relevant here too. The clearer the picture, the more effective this exercise will be.

This task may be considered a form of procrastination, but productive procrastination helps you understand the 'what' and 'why's'.

Once you have that clear in your head, think about what needs to be done based on the importance of it. When you go to your list and start taking action, set yourself a short time frame; for the next 20 minutes, that one task is all you will do. I have always found that once you get started, it is easier to keep going, and before you know it, you are ticking off that list and getting things done. Always set the time frame you are using as manageable.

Some people's working environment is critical, and they can't start working until their space or working area is clear, clean and tidy. If this is you, make sure you create that space in advance, the night before, and you can't use that as an excuse in the morning. If the ritual of tidying puts you into your headspace for work, then make that part of your list and start earlier.

The more we can plan ahead, set our next day up the night before, look at our list, know what we need to do, and then set up our space to limit the potential excuses for the next day.

Finding a way or environment that allows you to get the work done is essential. When I started writing this book, I needed to be away from my house and in a café where I didn't have good WiFi. The reviews and edits were slightly different; I found I didn't want to sit at my laptop so much, so I bought a notepad, and the 2nd edit started out handwritten, and the final drafts were done at my kitchen table in short 2 hours bursts or train commutes to Birmingham for training courses.

You will avoid some things because they bore you to tears or challenge you in unproductive ways. This is when you will really benefit from learning the art of delegation.

I have an assistant who uploads my podcasts each week and helps with background website layouts and design, so all I need to do is create the content. She also does other amazing technical stuff; I don't know what it is, I ask for things, and she makes it real. There is nothing I hate more than sitting at a computer waiting for websites to upload and moving between screens, and what takes me about 3 hours to do, she does in around 20 minutes. There is also the additional benefit that she holds me accountable, and when my content is not ready for her to upload, she is chasing me up – at that point, I need to stop procrastinating and get some work done. This is really working to your strengths.

Getting a coach or mentor is extremely valuable, depending on what you must do. Not only do you have a sounding board to bounce ideas off of, but you also have someone holding you accountable. There is a coach or planner for every area of your life.

Sometimes, you need to get away from everything to clear your head and chill out to make a better, more productive start later. Allow yourself to have these times, give yourself room to breathe and clear your head. Some of the best ideas come through meditation, a long walk, a bath, and going on holiday.
Changes in scenery and surrounding yourself with different people will always help you see things from a different perspective.

There is no point sitting in front of your laptop, freaking out that you have so much to do, scrolling through social media and getting nothing done. You are much better off stepping away, clearing your head and coming back later ready to go.

On the other side of that, though, as much as I want to give you permission to not beat yourself up all the time, there are times when you need to get a grip, put your phone away, switch off all distractions and do what needs to get done and deal with it.

This is your life, happiness, and responsibility to make it the best you can. Being pissed off with yourself and your excuses does not make you a happy human. Being pissed off with yourself can spur you into action and stop making excuses, so if you need to, listen to yourself for a minute, get pissed at your situation, then start listening to your inner warrior and take the action you need to get where you need to go.

Procrastination at its worst is stalling and holding back from whatever you want to achieve. Whether it is weight loss, finding romance, starting or pushing your business forward, moving to another country or sorting your shit, it's up to you to take responsibility.

All procrastination is, are you being controlling and wanting or needing everything to be perfect (this is said by a perfectionist in recovery who is working hard to change her ways). Taking that first step and letting go of control can be scary; change can be difficult and outright terrifying, especially when we have no idea what the outcome will be. A new job, a career change, a new relationship, a new country, a new lifestyle...

We must remember that change is also the most fantastic thing ever... Yes, it can be scary, but... a new job, a career change, a new relationship, a new country to live in, a new lifestyle... these can all fulfil your dreams and goals, create new exciting opportunities, and show you a whole new world of experience that you will never get if you continue to avoid change.

No one wants to or deserves to live an unhappy or unfulfilled life. If you are genuinely disappointed in your life, you need to be brave and make the decisions you need to make to be happy. Making the decision to end my marriage wasn't easy; that whole process took me to many unhappy places before I was truly happy again; most of that unhappiness was through my procrastination in dealing with my emotions. Ultimately if we had stayed together, we would have both been unhappy. Your decisions are more significant than that, or they're not; whatever they are, at the core of it is you and your happiness.

When you think about the universe and planets in their entirety, in the grand scheme of things, we are only on this planet for a short time, so really, we want to make what we have as happy, fun, enjoyable, and fulfilling as possible. Yes, that can be easier said than done... But you must be looking for something to be here and reading this book.

We need to live a life of fear of regret, not a fear of failure.

When you think about 'the end', no one gets to their deathbed and says, 'I really regret taking all those chances in life'. We never regret the chances we have taken; we only regret the chances we didn't take (the boy/girl you didn't speak to, the job you didn't apply for, the trip you didn't take...).

When we have these fears the wrong way around, we procrastinate and regret more... Missed conversations, opportunities, connections... 'If only I had just spoken to / said that / had a go....' When you give it a go, at least you know the outcome instead of assuming the result.

So how do we overcome this procrastination and fear of change and start embracing it?

Exercise
Like the previous exercise, start with a few big deep breaths in and out, and focus on your breath until you feel a sense of calm.

Then, I want you to look at where you are in your world. What is it specifically about your world that you don't like?
So often, we focus on the dream and don't think about the place we are at right now. Sometimes it's not that far from where you want to be, or it is so polar opposite that it propels you into action. Get right down to the tiny details. This isn't to put you in a bad mood but to get you to realise what you don't like.
Is it something you have control over?

What can be done to change it if it is within your control?

When you break down the specifics, one small aspect can bring you down. Change what you can.

If you are unhappy with your job, lifestyle, or image, change it or your perspective of it. There are so many people out there that have created businesses out of helping people make change.
Find someone who speaks your language in their videos or blog posts and gets what your problem is. It should feel like they are already inside your head, looking at the world through your eyes.

If you feel sluggish and distracted and could do with a boost to your energy levels – change what you are eating, make sure there are lots of healthy choices, make sure you are drinking enough fluids, and seek professional advice if you need it.

I know several people who read and listen to every personal development, self-help book, video, podcast, course, etc. They are gatherers of information; they never actually do anything with all the information they gather. You can read and listen to and agree with them all, but if you don't act and change something, nothing will change.

Be the one that makes the change and inspires other people. You need to start with one thing to make a difference.

Action
- Breathe
- Accept responsibility for your actions
- Be honest with yourself, always
- Give yourself a break
- Meditate
- Get over yourself, don't let your ego hold you back
- Understand that everyone has these same issues
- Takes some time to think about what it is you actually want (go back to your goals from chapter 3)
- Make a list, plan ahead and schedule in your time
- Take action
- Find an accountability buddy
- Find a coach or mentor that will help you
- Reward yourself for completing tasks

Rule #7

Love Yourself

Believe in Yourself

Although I believe that self-love and self-belief are two different things, they go hand in hand, and one is as important as the other, which is why I have put them together in one rule. You could have elements of one without the other, but they are much more powerful together.

When I think about self-love, I believe it's about looking after yourself physically, mentally, and emotionally, respecting yourself, putting yourself first, and filling your cup; remember that cup of water I talked about way back at the start. Self-belief has the confidence to love yourself.

I know many people who take a lot of care in their personal presentation but struggle with many other things. They are always well-presented but are unhappy with their weight, social life and/or relationship status. They have enough self-love to present themselves to the world in a particular way and enough self-belief to have awesome jobs, but it's not connecting to all areas of their life.

Something inside stops them from loving and believing enough in themselves.

You may be really fortunate to have people in your world who do believe in you and encourage you; that's great; start listening to them because not everyone has that kind of support around. The unfortunate thing is most of us, at some point, have had people put us down, embarrass us in public, or tell us we are 'too big for our boots', and that has been enough to plant the seed of doubt.

The name, 'self-belief', means you should be validated by the self rather than external sources. We go through life being validated by our parents, teachers, bosses, and partners when really, if we are living by our values, their opinion, lovely as it is to be externally validated, shouldn't be needed.

When we start to put things back together and rebuild our confidence, tuning in to the people praising us and tuning out of the ones that berate us takes awareness.

I have been very fortunate that my parents have always been supportive and encouraging; they stayed far enough back to let me make many mistakes and learn for myself but were also there when I needed them. At school, I was always under the radar, middle of the road, and generally disengaged. 12 years I dawdled through with only a couple of teachers that actually had me engaged and interested in their classes. I left high school not sure who I was, having no idea what I wanted to do and thinking I wasn't good at anything.

Even now, as a fully grown adult, loving what I do, I question my abilities and need to remind myself how far I have come and what I have achieved. It has taken time for me to stop continually looking outside for reassurance. I still gladly accept any constructive feedback from mentors. It is human nature to want someone to pat you on the head and tell you that you are doing a good job, and it does mean even more when you get it without looking for it.

Just before completing the first edition of this book, I was notified of being nominated for 2 different awards, one of them I shortlisted as Mentor of the Year with Business Women Scotland and the other as Best Pilates Instructor Glasgow with MoveGB, at the time of going to print I knew I didn't win the Mentor of the Year. I know that 2016 I won Best Pilates Instructor in Glasgow and have a lovely glass award on my shelf. I was really touched to be nominated and recognised for my hard work. They were awards I had been nominated for, not ones I had put myself forward for.

I am a big believer in constructive feedback; it's how we learn and grow, how we gain confidence and self-belief and allows us to be better next time. Over the last couple of years, I have become more confident and realise I know what I am talking about. I figure that a decade into a career I have immersed myself in, I must have more than sufficient knowledge (but know that I am always open to learning more).

I can't tell you with 100% certainty whether the self-belief encouraged self-love or the other way around, but I can tell you that over time, having worked through the content I shared with you in the previous rules, both have become stronger in me.

One particular fear I always had around self-belief and self-love was about coming across as arrogant. Who am I to think I am great at what I do?

I learned that the difference between arrogance and confidence is that arrogance is fuelled by insecurity, and there is an overcompensation to try and prove you know what you are about; there is a lack of willingness to listen to others.

Confidence is being secure in who you are and what you know and being willing to listen and grow. Once I understood this, I was less concerned about sharing my knowledge and skills.

You know what you know, share it and teach it with empathy. Sharing your knowledge and skills can help someone else. Why would you hold back from helping someone who needs you?

When you are prepared to put the work in, learn the skills you need, whether personal or professional, seek out the right mentors and coaches, ask for and take on board constructive feedback to help you grow and develop and also acknowledge your successes so far. You have every right to have confidence, self-love and self-belief. You will always be disappointed if you are always looking for perfection to validate self-belief.

I remember reading a post on Instagram that said:
'Good news.
You are perfect.
Everyone is.
Perfectly imperfect.
Embracing and accepting imperfections are all part of believing in and loving yourself. I mentioned earlier in the book that vulnerability is one of your greatest strengths.

If you believe in and love yourself enough, you can put something out there and accept that it's not 100% perfect. That doesn't mean that you don't need to put in any effort; everything you do should always be the best you can give at that moment. The first edition of this book wasn't perfect, and neither is the second, but I know that the books are works in progress and that I am the one being overly judgemental. I am sure that someone reading it will pick up on grammatical errors, have a better way of doing things, or have heard it all before. – I don't care (anymore). The feedback I have had from many is that it really helped change lives. It has changed lives because a reader has been inspired enough by something I said to trigger the motivation to change – that's what's important to me.

When we are striving for perfection, it creates stress, anxiety and exhaustion. As a recovering perfectionist, I can contest that.

You never feel like you are good enough or will ever be good enough; you set the bar high (which is a good thing to have high standards and expectations of yourself), but as soon as you get close, you put it up another 2 steps. By doing this, you are never allowing yourself to feel or enjoy the success of your achievements because you are always focused on the next step.

Stop for a moment and look over the last year at how far you have come. Life moves so quickly that we need to take time to appreciate our journey. We need to remember our achievements so quickly. I often have to refer to my social media photos or journal to see what I have done.

We all have things that we see in ourselves that we don't like (think back to the exercise from rule 3), but if someone looks at you, they don't see what you see. Things you may be self-conscious about (crooked teeth, chubby cheeks, lopsided smile, big butt) they will find endearing or not even notice. We are instinctively drawn to what we find attractive when we look at other people.

You will embrace your imperfections and make them your own; everyone else is too busy worrying about their imperfections to worry about yours*. You are only the most important person in the room to yourself. Make friends with yourself; how would you speak to your best friend? Speak to yourself with that same love and compassion.

* A short note on being judgemental, most often, when you find yourself judging someone else, you think about the motivation behind it. Is it because you are looking for validation about your insecurity that allows you to think or feel at least I am not as bad as them? More often than not, it is in there somewhere that you need to make you feel better. Notice when you do it yourself and call yourself out on it. It's an ugly habit to have. When someone is being judgemental to you, or you hear them, remember it's more about them than anyone else.

How much head space would you free up if you weren't judging yourself and thinking negatively about yourself all the time? How much love would you show yourself if you were to start putting yourself first (even just some of the time)?

Imagine getting up in the morning and looking in the mirror and thinking, 'Yip, you have got this, you are amazing' rather than 'hair is a riot', 'I'm too fat', 'my skin looks awful'. For many of you, this might seem out of reach. Start with 'you are enough'. I have this as a twice-daily reminder on my phone. You are enough, just the way you are.

Let's have a look at how you look after yourself.

What is the first thing you do when you get up?
Do you reach straight for the mobile phone to check emails / social media?
Make breakfast for someone else?
Look in the mirror and tell yourself how horrendous you look?
Start work?
Get other people up and ready?
Rush about? Roll out of bed and straight out the door?
When you wake up, do you feel like you switch on for everyone else, whether it's your partner, family, customers or boss/colleagues?

Learning self-love will let you be the first person you look after. Think how nice it will be to take some time to care for you first. It would help if you created a morning routine that is all about your own self-love and self-care. When you start the day right, it helps the rest fall into place (or at least gives you a better footing to deal with things that don't go the way you hoped).

Exercise

Create a morning routine. It needs to be something that works for you. Some suggestions:

Meditation (of some sort)

Movement (Yoga, stretching, walking, running, cycle)

Dry body brushing

Self-massage with warm oil

Shower/Washing

Tongue scraping

Dental hygiene – brush, floss, salt water mouthwash, oil pulling

Breakfast

You might need to set your alarm a little bit earlier, but once you feel the benefits of your routine, you will be glad of the time.

Now that we bring peace and time into your life, we want to build more confidence to go with the calm, loving you.

Think about the things you are least confident about right now, those that you shy away from doing or shift from one day To Do list to the next, hoping that they will act themselves, or they have been on there so long that you can bin that idea altogether.

Maybe it is going on a date, applying for a new job, starting your own business, getting your driving licence... Becoming competent at something is the best way to build confidence in anything.

Looking back at your life, how many things have you achieved, what skills have you built?

Even walking or reading would have started out as something you were incompetent at; over time, you would have become competent and gained confidence by building skills, practising, and learning from mistakes. In your job, you would have started out not knowing what you were doing; through training, learning, and taking action, you have built competence and confidence. You are not born with the skills you have now.

Exercise

Think about how you would like your regular dream day to unfold (either write your answers here or use your workbook journal pages):

How would I like each day to start?
What would I like to be focusing my energy and attention on?
What makes me feel happy?
What gets me jumping out of bed and looking forward to the day?
What makes me feel balanced and settled?
What state of mind would I like to be in while I work?
What other aspects of my life do I wish to pay more attention to?
If I was to make one change this week, what would it be?
What skills or experience do I have that I can use to help me move forward today?
What new skill do I need to learn to gain more competence?
Where or how do I get that skill?
Is it realistic for me to get it?

Once you have the answers to these questions, it should give a clearer understanding of what is needed to help you map out a plan. This plan should help you become more competent, with the outcome of confidence. You may already be competent but have been too scared to admit it to yourself through fear of judgement. Or maybe there are a couple of minor changes you want to make...

Competence + Confidence = Self-Belief
Self-Belief + Understanding + respect = Self-Love

Action

- Breathe
- Accept responsibility for your actions
- Be honest with yourself, always
- Give yourself a break
- Meditate
- Let go of being perfect
- Know that you are enough
- Work on your competence to be confident
- Know that confidence and arrogance are not the same thing
- Let go of judgement of yourself and others
- Make friends with yourself

Rule #8

If you really want the   cake,
have it

Food, glorious food. We are what we eat.

My relationship with food has changed a lot over the years. It was never a particularly significant relationship for many years, and I saw it as an inconvenience. I was a very fussy eater (and still am but much better than I was). I now understand the benefits of eating, particularly the food that nourishes my body and soul.

For many of the people I work with, health or weight loss is initially one of their main goals and, more often than they realise, is an area of their life that they self-sabotage in.

I also know through experience working with many people over the years that food issues are a thing, even if they don't have a weight issue. Just about everyone I have ever spoken to knows exactly what I am talking about when I mention emotional eating.

In case you don't recognise that term, emotional eating is what we do when we are: stressed, sad, happy, angry, avoiding emotion, pissed off, hurt, rejected, anxious, depressed, bored etc.

It's any time that you eat when you are not actually hungry. What you are doing is distracting yourself from a situation with food. This usually involves indulging in foods that are not healthy, in large volumes, eaten unconsciously (without thinking and automatically), e.g. when you are watching TV eating a bag of crisps, you suddenly realise they are all gone, and you don't remember eating any of them. It often can involve entire packets of biscuits, cakes, tubs of ice cream, family bags of crisps and bottles of wine with a 'fuck it' or 'I don't care anymore, the world can kiss my fat ass' attitude.

Now, where this stems from is not our fault or our parent's fault, but it is our parent's responsibility when they (entirely innocently) conditioned us to see food as a reward or comfort when we were young. It probably happened with them too.

We were given sweets if we were good to reward us, we got them when we were crying to keep us quiet or comfort us, or it was used as a bargaining tool to create desired behaviours. And then there were your grandparents and extended family filling you with cakes, biscuits, sweets because you were at your grans or aunties as a 'treat'.

Apologies to the parents who have never used food as a reward, comfort or bargaining tool, but it does happen widely.

And I can't forget to mention the marketing companies who constantly show us images of people happy and relaxed while eating bars of chocolate, having the best fun while drinking fizzy juice, how cool you are for drinking certain liqueurs, it's all sexy, relaxed, seductive and happy...

These emotional triggers make us believe we need these foods and drinks in our diets.

Other things that run through our minds:

'I have been good all week, so I deserve....' 'I am sad, so I will bloody well eat what I want.'
'I can afford to have this now; we didn't have the money when I was young,
'the man/woman in the ad is so sophisticated/ beautiful when she is eating/drinking... It will make me that way too.

With all this in mind, discussing it in this book is appropriate.

How many fad diets have you tried for those of you who have food or weight issues (even if you would like to look better and lose a couple of pounds)?

You might not even want to start thinking about this, but how much money have you spent over the years on shakes, pills, tea, books, and DVD, and you seem to be far from your goals?
Maybe you are even further away from them?!

If you go into a bookshop or type diet book into Amazon, thousands of books promise you the perfect body, guaranteed results and super-fast changes that may or may not be biologically impossible for you to achieve.

The supplement industry is the same. Tubs of all sorts of concoctions promising you to slim down, burn fat faster or bulk up.

The thing to remember is, if any of them actually worked, then there would not be so many options on the shelves and not increasing numbers of people with health issues related to weight gain.

I read an article in a magazine once from an economist who reported that entire industries would collapse if every woman in the USA and Canada stopped buying beauty and diet products for a week. These industries and their marketing teams pray on our insecurities and emotions to get us consuming optimistically. Women used to be the primary target market; more recently, we have seen many products rebranded and sold to men as the cult of the bodybuilder image is spread as being a healthy look for men. Bodybuilding is not a sport, and extreme shape is not healthy or healthily attained by 99% of the general population. A small (maybe 1%) population achieves this effortlessly.

My advice to every single person:
Stop 'dieting', following the latest fad, or taking the latest miracle pill – removing food groups from your diet doesn't work; you need protein, fat and carbs from 'real' food. Neither does it replace food with shakes. You might get a short-term result, but it seriously damages your long-term health. Try not to think of foods as 'good' and 'bad'; food is food, and you want to eat it to nourish your body, mind and soul.

Eat mindfully. Taking time to sit and eat a meal instead of throwing food down our necks on the run, eating in the car en route to somewhere, or watching TV while we eat. When we are distracted, we don't register what we are eating, and we often don't chew our food enough, meaning that our stomach isn't ready to digest the food, and it hasn't been broken down enough before hitting our stomach. This causes significant health problems when undigested food gets stuck in your system, releasing toxins into your system. When food that isn't broken down enough passes through, the nutrients can't be absorbed, and our body can't do the needed job. There has been a massive increase in people suffering from IBS & IBD in recent years. Chewing your food might not prevent it, but it will make life easier. Turn off the TV, and put away your laptop and phone. If you need background noise (I am not a fan of hearing people chew), put some slow-paced music in the background. Sit at the table if you have one. Use your knife and fork, but put them down between mouthfuls. Wait to load up your fork, ready to go in as soon as you swallow. Chew your food at least 20 times, get the saliva working, get the enzymes needed for digestion switched on, make the task in your tummy easier, and hopefully reduce indigestion or heartburn. Enjoy your meal, every mouthful.

Learn about food and what works for you. Educate yourself and do some self-experimentation. This will mainly take time and be trial and error (don't learn from magazines, every month, they change their mind, and I have even seen contradicting advice within one article). It's a minefield of information. Stick with lots of fresh veggies, fruit, good carbs in the form of oats, rice, veg, lean protein in the form of good quality meat, fish, eggs, tofu, beans & pulses, and fats from coconut oils, butter (not margarine), olive oils, avocados, oily fish, nuts, seeds, nut butter and cold pressed oils. The more natural you can eat, the better.

Please pay attention, listen to your body to how your body responds to the food it is being fed. If you are getting a lot of gas and wind, you need to bring some heat into your digestive system – fresh ginger tea before eating can be really beneficial.

Notice your energy levels after eating if you are lethargic, have brain fog, itchy skin etc. Maybe the food you are eating doesn't agree with you. Some people struggle to digest salads (they are not a healthy meal for everyone).

Think of it as creating a lifestyle and being realistic about the changes, sorting one thing at a time, and integrating it with your life. An all-out overhaul is too much for most people and will create a backlash when it gets too much, and then you feel like a failure. Small manageable changes. If you have been eating Coco Pops for breakfast, your first change is to Rice Krispies or cornflakes if oats or eggs don't cut it.

Create a healthy first mindset as your aim for success. Eat food that makes you feel good inside and out. Food should nourish your heart and soul. If you eat something and instantly feel guilty... Why are you eating it? If you eat something that makes you bloat... Why are you eating it? If you eat something that makes your skin break out... Why are you eating it? You can see where I am going with this. Think about how you feel both mentally and physically. If you eat cake and love every mouthful, and you feel good after eating it, then there is no need to never eat cake.

Be around people that will help educate you and support you and your goals. Those friends that take the piss or tell you that you need to let your hair down are only doing it because they don't have the same goals as you, or you make them feel guilty because they know they should be taking better care of themselves. You either need to have great support or be strong-minded to stick to it when the people closest to you are not on board.

Find activities and exercise that you enjoy and mix them up from time to time. If you are not achieving your goals, you may need to change your approach – get help if needed. Going to the gym and doing fitness classes is not for everyone. Try different things to see what you enjoy. There are loads of adult sports teams, walking, running, and cycling groups around, and many are free to join. Just about every type of exercise class is available online, either free or through paid subscriptions.

Understand why there are things you don't want to have in your diet. Processed cane sugar is poison in your body; it can cause excess belly fat, make you moody and break your skin out, and has been linked to obesity and many cancers. Too much alcohol (another poison) slows down the digestive system making you hold more fat, and you usually eat a week's worth of junk food in the morning to get over the hangover. Processed food has a whole host of things added to it to make it taste good and be cheap to make; when items are far removed from their natural state, your body struggles to use them, and they have little to no nutrients to nourish your body and soul.

Keep well hydrated; with water, herbal tea, green tea, and freshly made veg juices. It is recommended you drink around 2 litres of fluid a day; if you are always inside with heating or air conditioning, these will dry you out more, so you need more fluid, likewise if you are active for most of the day. Regular small sips of fluid all day are much better than glugging gallons in one go and then needing to pee it all out 20 mins later. Top tip, have water at room temperature, and if you do find you are peeing a lot, a tiny pinch of sea salt in the water (not enough to taste) will help keep it in your body to be absorbed. If, for medical reasons, you are on a low-sodium diet, this would not be recommended.

Get good quality sleep. This has been a major player in my Crohn's healing journey (there will be an entire chapter on it in my next book). It would help if you had a good nighttime routine. Turn off the laptop / TV at least 1 hour before bed (the blue light from the screen messes with the release of melatonin (sleep hormone) and keeps you awake longer. Blue light filters and glasses are available but don't cancel out enough to use them as your validation to keep using your screen before bed. Chill out, bathe, read, meditate, focus on your breathing, making it slow and steady, and make a bedtime drink. I love nighttime teas or hot cacao (made with coconut milk and a dash of maple syrup).

Reduce your stress levels – Go back to the rule on stress; what else can you do to remove stress from your life? When you are stressed, your digestive system doesn't work correctly. Spending a minute before eating to focus on my breathing and taking long, slow breaths for 6-10 repetitions calms me and has helped the digestive process.

Make a treat a treat – I don't actually like the word 'treat'. This is because what we associate with the term is things like Chocolate biscuits, cakes, crisps, take away food. Are these really 'treats'? A treat is nourishing and loving and makes us feel fantastic. These are all just convenience junk foods rather than a treat. Is fuelling your body with toxins actually a self-loving 'treat'? For the most part, they are part of daily life rather than an every now and again. Resetting your understanding and connection with these types of food will allow you to have them as a choice, checking in with yourself; is this really what I want?

I will not tell you that I don't eat any of that; I do. It's something that I have been thinking about a lot when I think about the associations we have with it.
If you eat it, do it guilt-free because you know it is a conscious choice? What is better: hiding behind the fridge door while you inhale half a cake feeling guilty, hoping you don't get caught or sitting in a café with friends enjoying a chat and a bit of cake?

Once we improve our relationship with food and ourselves, we begin to feel and look better. Always question your actions. Is this for comfort or pleasure and health? Our skin is clearer, we have loads of energy, we sleep better, and as a bonus, we look better. When the focus comes away from weight loss, what we look like to how we feel inside, our mood, and our energy, the stress of being in the 'right' shape disappears.

We will never resemble the people on the covers of magazines (they don't even look like that thanks to Photoshop), and really, if you knew the effort, stress, and unhappiness they go through to look like that, you would realise that to be really lean with your 6 pack showing is not a healthy way to be. Athletes look the way they do because their job is to be the best at whatever sport they compete in; that is their full-time job. They train for hours every single day. We can only look like us; we are all different shapes and sizes, which we have no control over.

What we have is responsibility and control over how we treat our bodies. We are fully responsible for what we eat and how much we move; accepting that responsibility can be tricky. There are no shortcuts; there is no magic pill. When you are on board with the rest of this book, this will all seem so much easier.

Exercise

Now that we are starting to understand how food can benefit us, it will be beneficial for you to begin to track what you are eating and how your food makes you feel. Start with a 3-day tracker, including 2 working days and 1 non-working day. You can use an app, your online calendar or download a Food and Mood diary template from www.iamjenwilson.com/resources .

Remember to track food, drinks and portion size. How you identify portion size is entirely up to you, it can be by weight if you have that information or handful sizes, using your hand as a gauge. Whatever works better for you.

With your moods, you are looking for energy levels to increase, decrease, irritability, increase in happiness, decrease in satisfaction, ability to make decisions, cravings, sleep quality, how you feel when you wake up and any noticeable bloating.
The more detail you take down, the more precise your picture will be. If you need more than 3 days to give you a good enough view, continue for 7 days, but don't get obsessed with it. Use it occasionally to keep you focused, aware and on track.

So what do we do with that information? Depending on your goal and what you notice from your diary, you can start fine-tuning your lifestyle to make your food work. If you see slumps in the day, what have you eaten? If there is bloating or irritability, try removing certain foods and continue to monitor. Sugar, dairy, and wheat are often good places to start removing as these are what a standard diet is overloaded with. You need a good 4 weeks without adding one in for a week to see what happens before you add another.

For further nutrition coaching, I have a programme specifically designed to increase your knowledge and help you work towards making your eating work for you. Contact me at jen@iamjenwilson.com for more information.

Action

- Breathe
- Accept responsibility for your actions
- Be honest with yourself, always
- Give yourself a break
- Meditate
- Stop dieting
- Eat mindfully
- Learn about food and how it makes you feel
- Think of it as creating a lifestyle and be realistic
- Create a mind-set with your goals and health as your aim
- Be around supportive people
- Find activities / exercise that you enjoy
- Understand the why's of food you are eliminating
- Keep well hydrated
- Get good sleep
- Reduce your stress levels
- Make a treat a treat

Rule #9

Let go

'It's *your life; these are your goals. You control your happiness. Work hard, be honest, be kind, and love yourself*' Jen Wilson, Creator and Founder of Warrior Woman Project® (yes, me).

The first edition of this book was done alongside the creation of my programme Warrior Woman Project®; the second edition was created for the men who wanted 9 Rules to Sort Their Shit but didn't want to become Warrior Women.

I thought long and hard about what I wanted the book's outcome to be. I also considered what the values of someone reading and working through this book might have.

These are the values that I see in every human, maybe you have these on your list from Rule 1, or they weren't ones that particularly jumped out at you. Perhaps you haven't realised that you have these values, or maybe you have not quite tapped into them just yet (remember there is no hard and fast rule around these):
- Ability to let go
- Courage
- Determination
- Strength
- Freedom
- Warrior
- Love

It doesn't matter if your values list looks entirely different for this list. Some of these values you feel you still need to work on; maybe from working through this book, you have realised that these are actually some of your values.

My definition of each differs totally from yours (which is absolutely okay).

When you decide to let go, whether out of fear, anger, or control, you tap into your courage, feel a sense of freedom and will feel happier. To let go of something means that it will no longer consume you. When you let go of pain or forgive someone who has hurt you, it is you who benefits from that letting go. Think about the times you have held on to negative emotions; I am sure they won't have made you feel free or happy. If anything, you will have felt more fearful, angrier or out of control. I was once told by a wise woman (my senior lecturer at college MaryAnn), 'Control the controllable and let go of the rest'. You are the only controllable.

The word courage comes from the heart. You can't be courageous unless you feel in your heart, taking risks and letting go. There will always be some element of risk (or indeed a feeling of risk).

Have you ever considered changing a situation worse than the experience and outcome? We always think things will be more dramatic or challenging than they actually are.

Determination is the ability to get back up each time you fall, not give up on yourself, and have faith in your courage.

Strength comes from learning about yourself, being vulnerable, accepting yourself as you are right now and knowing that you can make any changes you want.

Freedom is looking in the mirror and loving the person looking back exactly as you are. Not a few pounds lighter, not when you get the new job, not any other time than right now.

Warrior is the fighter inside who will not stand for anyone putting you down, causing harm or making you feel small. You will do everything in your power to be healthy, happy and live a life you are delighted to wake to.

Love is the purest of it all. You see it, feel it, want it for everyone.
There are no caveats; pure love for you and everyone around you.

How does all this fit in with letting go?

If you are in a job you hate and you want to start your own business, the thought of not having job security is scary, but when you actually take the step and end up doing something you absolutely love doing, you will find happiness that can't be bought with money.

You can think about a time when you changed jobs and couldn't have been happier with that change. You left the security of a job you knew and the people you were familiar with to something where you were starting from scratch again, learning a new system, possibly in a new location, and with a new team of workmates. Your new job and environment were excellent.

Sometimes a change is as good as a rest.

If you have been single for years and are very happy being single but would like to be in a relationship, the thought of finding that relationship is scary. Then you hear about other people's dating disaster experiences that put you off even trying. The comfort of being single can be just too appealing. (This could be the same in the opposite; maybe being 'comfortable' but not happy in a relationship that isn't really what you want is more straightforward than facing a life of being single).

Whether you are looking to be in a relationship or are already in one, you need to be open and accepting of the relationship. A relationship does not complete you; it should complement you. If you have been single for some time, you need to be happy and comfortable being on your own before you enter into a relationship, or you could be settling for something that does not fit in the long run (and leave you feeling miserable and thinking relationships are not for you).

I speak from experience here. I was very comfortable being on my own, then one day, this man appeared in my life through a chance meeting in Tesco. To cut a long story short, a friend is getting involved to move things in the right direction, and somehow he fits, and it all feels amazing. I know that it may or may not last; either way, I have let go of trying to control anything; I am taking each day exactly as it comes and enjoying it for what it is.

The thing to remember when it comes to bringing someone else into your life, whether it is a romantic interest or a new friend or a business partner, is that you need to be happy with who you are and what you want in your life so you can be independent in a codependent relationship. If you are trying to fill a void or are looking for someone else to make you happy, complete you, or fix you, then you are in the fast lane to having the wrong people around you. That's not to say that people can't be there for you and support and help you, but your motives for being there must be sincere to your needs and match your values.

It is the same thought process if you are in an unhappy relationship. Why are you sad? What is not happening for it to be happy? Just going through the exercises in this book will be enough for you to realise who you are and what you want, and that can change the dynamics of that relationship (this, again, can be friendships or family, not just romantic). Sometimes the dynamics change for the better, and you create something that works better, and sometimes you need to walk away because it is the best thing for both parties (like my divorce and other connections I cut ties with over the years).

This courage gives you determination to keep going, to be strong and move towards your dreams and happiness. Taking the time to be clear on who you are and what you want can make life so much easier to navigate through.

You can stand up and say 'Yes' to what you want and 'No' to what you don't want. You have confidence in yourself to have the strength in this powerful knowledge of you.

This gives you freedom and happiness. You know that through your hard work and honesty throughout the exercises in this book, you have sorted your shit out (and don't stress if you read that last statement and are thinking, 'Well, not quite yet', you are a work in progress. I am a work in progress. We are done when we are done (last breath done).

Exercise

I have created an audio download for you to help you let go. This is a lovely and very effective meditation to help you let go of stresses and tensions that you might be holding on to. To download this final exercise, head over to www.iamjenwilson.com/resources

Action

- Breathe
- Accept responsibility for your actions
- Be honest with yourself, always
- Give yourself a break
- Meditate
- Let go (use the download)
- Use your courage
- Allow yourself freedom
- Love yourself

Conclusion
and
Moving Forward

What happens now?

Firstly CONGRATULATIONS for getting through the book all the way to the end! Not everyone will have reached this point, so be proud of yourself for this completion. It shows absolute determination and strength of character to push through. I know that some of the exercises will have challenged you (they challenge me too, but that's the point).

If you have had a read-through and have yet to do the exercises, I beg you to go back and do the exercises; otherwise, all you will have done is read another self-help book and not change.

Remember you can get your 9 Rules to Sort Your Shit Workbook with spaces mapped out for the exercises in this book.

Thank you for making it all the way through, and I genuinely hope you got as much out of the process as I have done over the last few years. Rebuilding my life and finding confidence in myself and my abilities has been a journey and a half, and it's not over yet. It's not always easy, and there will be slip-ups, diversions, road bumps, challenges and life getting in the way occasionally. The more you stay focused on yourself and what you want, the more resilient and confident you will become.

After the release of the first edition of this book in December 2016, I got really sick; in March 2017, I was diagnosed with Crohn's disease. I realised during my recovery that while writing this book, I had not followed my own 9 Rule. I had some major shit to sort (pun intended). In going back through the rules and working on myself, I healed. I am not claiming that the rules healed me, but they set the conditions for me to heal. Remember that you can try as many things as you like in life.

Don't think of anything as a failure; instead, think of it as confirmation of something wrong for you. I have 'failed' at many things (school, businesses, marriage, friendships, relationships...). There are so many things that I could probably write a whole book just on discovering what wasn't for me.

You will get to where you want to be because I know you want to (you read this book for a reason and got this far), and when you have worked out what it is you want, the planning and action phase just put all the pieces in place ready for you to take action.

Then you take the action; I have faith in you
Big love,
Jen x

PS. If you have enjoyed this book, can you please leave me a review over on Amazon, share about it on social media, pass it on, or recommend it to your friends, family, work colleagues, or anyone that you think would benefit from the book, even buy them all as birthday and Christmas gifts?

References

Colonel Chris Hadfield – The Sky is not the Limit (talk)

Brené Brown – The Power of Vulnerability (book)

ACKNOWLEDGEMENTS

I am still eternally grateful to Kim and Sinclair of Indie Authors World, without them the first book would never have made it to print and digital never mind the second edition.

To Kris my partner in life who not only encourages me to do whatever I like but puts up with my nonsense and has stuck by me during my time of ill health.

The NHS for their speedy diagnosis, care and ongoing monitoring me.

All the readers and supporters of the first edition, I thank you and love you.

To the Universe for its continual shaking and moving to get me on the right path. I am listening, I promise.

ABOUT THE AUTHOR

Jen Wilson, author of Become a Warrior Woman, 9 Rules to Sort   Your Shit, and creator of Warrior Woman Project® has been   working in the wellness industry since 2009. She created the   Warrior Woman Project® back in 2014 after identifying that much of her own journey resonated with other women who were feeling stuck or

lost in their own worlds.

Then in 2017 after being diagnosed with Crohn's disease she realised that the 'health' journey she was on was more damaging that it was doing her good. Jen helps her clients work out what it is they want in life, who they truly are and what they are truly capable of, and work from a place of self-love.

With a background in fitness, nutrition, NLP, massage, Pilates, Yoga, meditation, Reiki and coaching she has a wide and varied approach to helping the world heal.

Thank You

Hey, it's Jen here, I just wanted to say thank you so much for taking the time to read my book. It means so much to me that you firstly bought it, but also read it. If you enjoyed the book it would mean the world to me if you could spare a couple of minutes to go over to Amazon and leave a review. It helps other people find the book and helps encourage them to make a purchase.

When you self-publish a book like I have there is no marketing team or publishing house with a budget to help get my book in front of people so all the help we can get makes a massive difference.

I am a real person, doing what she can to help as many people as possible and you can be part of that too.

Please reach out to me if there is anything I can do for you.

Big love

Jen x

Connect with Jen

jen@iamjenwilson.com

Website:

www.iamjenwilson.com

Instagram

www.instagram.com/iam.jenwilson

Facebook:

www.facebook.com/iamjenwilson

YouTube

www.youtube.com/iamjenwilson